X3 CO-GED+109

The Teaching Assistant's Guide to the Basic Course

Katherine Grace Hendrix
University of Memphis

THOMSON
———✳———™
WADSWORTH

Australia • Canada • Mexico • Singapore • Spain • United Kingdom • United States

COPYRIGHT © 2000 Wadsworth, a division of Thomson Learning, Inc. Thomson Learning™ is a trademark used herein under license.

ALL RIGHTS RESERVED. No part of this work covered by the copyright hereon may be reproduced
or used in any form or by any means—graphic, electronic, or mechanical, including but not limited to photocopying, recording, taping, Web distribution, information networks, or information storage and retrieval systems—without the written permission of the publisher.

Printed in the United States of America
3 4 5 6 7   07 06 05 04 03

Printer: Malloy Incorporated

ISBN: 0-534-56778-9

For more information about our products,
contact us at:
Thomson Learning Academic Resource Center
1-800-423-0563

For permission to use material from this text,
contact us by:
Phone: 1-800-730-2214
Fax: 1-800-731-2215
Web: http://www.thomsonrights.com

Wadsworth/Thomson Learning
10 Davis Drive
Belmont, CA 94002-3098
USA

Asia
Thomson Learning
5 Shenton Way #01-01
UIC Building
Singapore 068808

Australia/New Zealand
Thomson Learning
102 Dodds Street
Southbank, Victoria 3006
Australia

Canada
Nelson
1120 Birchmount Road
Toronto, Ontario M1K 5G4
Canada

Europe/Middle East/South Africa
Thomson Learning
High Holborn House
50/51 Bedford Row
London WC1R 4LR
United Kingdom

Latin America
Thomson Learning
Seneca, 53
Colonia Polanco
11560 Mexico D.F.
Mexico

Spain/Portugal
Paraninfo
Calle/Magallanes, 25
28015 Madrid, Spain

Dedication

Valerian Keith Hendrix, Sr.

Table of Contents

Chapter 1 1
Overview of Graduate Teaching Assistant Experience 1
    Socialization 2
    Teacher Concerns 3
    Pedagogical Knowledge 4
    Cited Readings...7
Chapter 2 9
Surviving the First Week of Classes 9
    Department Expectations...9
    Emphasizing the First Week of Teaching...10
    Cited Readings..16
Chapter 3 17
Designing a Syllabus 17
    Identifying Information..18
    Course Description 19
    Policies 19
    Grading System 19
    Daily Class Schedule and Assignment Overview...............................20
    Student Resources..20
Chapter 4 21
Knowing Yourself as Classroom Teacher 21
    Facing Learned Biases 21
    Graduate Teaching Assistants of Color...25
    The Context of Your Teaching..27
    Recommended Readings..30
Chapter 5 33
Strategies for Non-Native English Speaking GTAs 33
    Before Classes Begin..33
    First Week of Classes..34
    During Class 34
    Other Information 34
    Recommended Readings..36
Chapter 6 37
Lecturing and Group Discussion 37
    Lecturing...37
    Group Discussion 39
    Cited Readings..42
    Recommended Readings..43
Chapter 7 45

Grading Oral Performance **45**
    Formal Presentations 45
    Classroom Management 46
    Facilitating Speaking Days 47
    Addressing Communication Anxiety 48
    Grading 49
    Returning Grades 51
    Small Group Work 52
    Cited Readings 54
    Recommended Readings 55
Chapter 8 .... **57**
Discipline and Motivation **57**
    Unprepared Students 57
    Talkative Students 58
    Outbursts 59
    Managing Sensitive Topics 61
    Plagiarism 62
    Cited Readings 64
    Recommended Readings. 64
Chapter 9 .... **65**
Record Keeping **65**
    Creating a Gradebook 65
    Final Grade Computation 67
    Grade Appeals 68
    Creating a Class Profile 69
Chapter 10 .... **71**
The Rewards of Self Assessment **71**
    Formal Assessment 71
    Reflective Teaching and Self Assessment 72
    Cited Readings 74
    Recommended Readings 75
Campus Contacts **76**
Index **77**

Preface

Most standard dictionaries refer to art as a conscious, nonscientific arrangement of sounds, movement, forms, and colors which positively affect the senses. Artists are individuals who create works of art or who engage in some form of work as if it were art. While there are pedagogical assumptions about the nature of knowledge and how to best facilitate learning, no one can provide you with an exact set of specifications to ensure a successful learning environment.

Learning environments are artistically (not scientifically) co-created between students and teacher/learners. While the artist must know the fundamentals such as lighting, colors, depth, and technique, the ability to see and share nuance varies according to the capabilities and heart of each artist.

This teaching guide is designed as a conversation between the two of us while introducing you to the fundamentals of teaching. Think of your students as a palette of colors. As you work with the colors and tools available to you, it will take time, initiative, and creativity to learn pleasing combinations. Over time, instead of following a series of steps and rote memorization, you will learn style and perspective. Ideally, you will come to understand and appreciate the beauty of teaching.

I welcome you into the honorable, artistic profession of teaching and a life full of learning.

K. G. Hendrix

Chapter 1
Overview of Graduate Teaching Assistant Experience

In the early 1900s when graduate fellowships became linked with campus service, scholars considered questions as to whom graduate fellowships should be awarded, what responsibilities should entail, and whether the recipients should be trained. The answers regarding appropriate classroom training ranged from the belief that effective teaching would result from "secur[ing] capable men as graduate students" to those who believed that a strong research background led to effective classroom teaching (Gray, 1930, p. 80).

Even in the 21st century, post-secondary scholars continue to address these same questions regarding graduate teaching assistants (GTAs). Institutional training programs range from those conferring complete freedom (no training) to those mandating conformity across all sections of the same course (Nadler, 1985; Trank, 1990). Departments which do not offer training fundamentally operate on the belief "that bright people learn to teach by teaching" (Allen & Rueter, 1990, p. ix) whereas those offering training perceive the need for GTAs to take time for self-reflection as they learn how to teach and, in some cases, prepare for a career in the professoriate (Ryan & Martens, 1989; Svinicki, 1995–96).

Inexperienced GTAs—including those who have transferred to a new institution, and those being assigned to new course preparations—normally experience self concerns where they are preoccupied with academic survival, managing their classroom credibility, and maintaining control in their classrooms (Darling & Dewey, 1990). As a result, while it is important to develop content knowledge, it is equally important to reduce the levels of uncertainty, fear, and stress which you might experience after being assigned to teach. One way of reducing your anxiety level and increasing your confidence is to acquire information to assist with the process of socializing into your new role as GTA.

This teaching guide provides information on how to design and conduct your courses. In addition, you are urged to explore your cultural assumptions and self-image as a person and classroom teacher. Every aspect of who you are, including your personality traits and upbringing, have the potential to influence your teaching philosophy, style, and interaction with students. This first chapter provides an overview with the focus on (a) defining socialization, (b) identifying three categories of novice teacher concern, and (c) increasing awareness of pedagogically-based discussions and debates within the discipline.

Socialization

Socialization involves acquiring the characteristics (for example, beliefs, mannerisms and values) of the group you wish you join. It is a process of learning how to think, speak, and behave in ways consistent with other group members which, of course, occurs over time and with much practice. You must learn at least two roles—graduate student and novice teacher—while simultaneously maintaining other roles such as family member, spouse and friend. Staton and Darling (1989) discuss three typical communication strategies: passive, active, and interactive behavior. You will likely use one or more of these strategies to assist you in obtaining information in uncertain situations.

The passive strategy involves observation rather than direct contact with the source of the needed information. Using the passive strategy, you might linger after a meeting to hear what the basic course director may be saying to another GTA or you might watch, from down the hall, as a more experienced GTA consults with a student outside the classroom. When using active strategies, you might engage in conversation but not with the direct source of the needed information. In such a case, for example, you might try to obtain information from the departmental secretary or the office of campus registrar. Finally, you could choose to be interactive and to converse with the primary source of information. Sometimes the conversation with your primary source takes place after you have learned what to expect by observing or asking others. At times, you may prefer the active strategy where you seek advice from another GTA instead of your basic course director or departmental chair. Darling and Dewey (1990) refer to experienced GTAs as "interpretive guides" who can assist you in recognizing and understanding the cultural milieu of your department and campus. However, I would caution you to obtain information from several of your colleagues in order to operate with a more holistic rather than myopic view of your department and what is expected of you. Consider that these definitions, and others in this guide, are culturally bound and, as such, reflect a Westernized world view. It is conceivable that what is defined here as *passive* would be viewed as an active choice in other cultures.

The socialization process involves learning your roles, both as graduate student and teacher, in your department's classrooms. Being assigned a role implies a set of expectations regarding your behavior and, according to Galvin (1990), there are at least five role functions associated with class-room teaching. Galvin says that classroom teachers are normally expected to provide content expertise, managed learning, evaluation and feedback, student socialization, and personal models. The role of *teacher* carries the expectation that you will: (a) know the course content: (b) teach effectively in a supportive environment; (c) fairly assess your students: (d) introduce your students to discipline and alternate views of the world, and (e) develop interpersonal relationships and serve as a role model of a respectful, engaged discussant. Reading this guide and talking with others about your teaching can help facilitate socialization into your role as teacher.

The process of socializing into your role as teacher will not be stress free. Your department training and time you spend in preparation will positively influence your experience in the classroom. Communicating with others, reviewing articles and books on teaching and culture, and preparing for your classes will significantly reduce the unknown and, thereby, reduce your stress. The more you know about what is expected of you—and the normal phases of anxiety experienced by new teachers—the more control you will sense over your circumstances. Eventually, you will gain confidence and enjoy your opportunity to facilitate the learning process of your students as well as your own. Doubtless, you will be nervous as you begin your first few weeks of teaching. In the following section, I will review the literature on typical teacher concerns.

Teacher Concerns

Fuller categorizes the thoughts of new teachers as representing self, task, and impact concerns (1969; Fuller and Parsons, 1972). Self concerns preoccupy new teachers with issues of maintaining credibility, classroom control, and survival in their new role. Task concerns are related to mastering particular aspects of teaching such as lecturing, facilitating group discussions, and so forth. Impact concerns generally develop last (for example, toward the end of the first year of teaching) and represent a teacher's concern for student learning. These three concerns have also been identified among GTAs (Darling & Dewey, 1990) and even among experienced professors teaching new preparations (Staton-Spicer & Marty-White, 1981). These concerns will also likely manifest themselves in experienced GTAs who have been accepted to a new institution. Even with experience, our anxiety and fear of the unknown increase as our environment changes.

GTA concerns are not without merit, and so, it is natural to be concerned about your position as a GTA rather than viewing it as a casual responsibility. Allen and Reuter indicate that you must learn to function in the "highly political environment [of college departments typically] consisting of strata of prestige and influence" (1990, p. ix). Consistent with this perspective, McKeachie notes that GTAs should determine the role of a faculty member not only in their department but at the institution, as well, because "a course cannot be divorced from the total college or university culture" (1994, p. 5). Second, your use of dress, professional behavior, and the appropriate levels of authority may influence whether you are perceived merely as a student or as a *real teacher* (Willer, 1993). Professionalism can "include organization, preparation, maturity, self-confidence, fairness, handling responsibility, and owning behavior" (Burkel-Rothfuss & Fink, 1993, p. 93). And, third, you must prove yourself capable of simultaneously handling your roles as both teacher and advanced learner.

Remember you are not alone. Newly hired faculty in your department— whether they are new graduates or experienced faculty who have relocated to your campus—experience anxiety. Menges (1996) notes that research reveals the following five negative feelings experienced by junior faculty members: anxiety, pressure, isolation, personal tension, and dissonance regarding work rewards. In short, novice teachers are stressed as they learn their new roles and the corresponding expectations.

This guide is designed to provide the information you need to reduce your self and task concerns. These concerns are immediate in new teachers and I encourage you to acknowledge and address them. The following chapters discuss how to prepare yourself to reduce your fear of embarrassing yourself by handling your class inappropriately or not knowing how to teach a particular lesson.

In addition to content knowledge, curriculum development, and classroom management, you must be aware of different scholarly perspectives regarding communication education. Communication education refers to studying and developing theories and applications regarding how to best teach communication courses. Perspectives pertaining to pedagogy are an intricate part of communication education. Pedagogy basically refers to principles of instruction which facilitate effective teaching and student learning. Your familiarity with classroom pedagogy will increase your understanding of what is perceived as knowledge and how you can promote knowledge acquisition, which is the essence of learning.

Pedagogical Knowledge

Sprague (1990) says that four basic educational goals include transmitting cultural knowledge, developing students' intellectual skills, providing students with careers, and reshaping societal values. As you reflect on your education, perhaps you can see that your teachers operated with one or more of these goals in mind. You may also determine during what stages of your education, your teachers focused on the psychomotor (manipulative and motor skills such as holding a pencil and coloring within lines), affective (feelings), and cognitive (knowledge) aspects of learning. As graduate level Communication major, you likely operate primarily within the realm of the cognitive. However, as you teach a required general education course in your department, it is useful to understand the importance of setting goals and objectives which address both cognitive and affective dimensions of learning. Your students, especially non-majors, will request information about the relevance of your course content. By familiarizing yourself with these dimensions of learning, you will discover how to design goals (what you want your students to accomplish or understand) and objectives (the steps to move your students toward designated goals). As a novice teacher, create goals and objectives for yourself in regard to each of your lesson plans and, in general, your teaching.

Sprague (1990) says that even experienced teachers often skip the process of establishing course goals. Unarticulated goals fail to assist instructors and their students in maximizing the learning process. One challenge associated with the goal-setting process is to recognize that identity is constituted in communication. As a result, we must be careful not to use our power (even GTAs have some power) to negate the identity of diverse students by being overly critical of their language or demeanor. Finesse— and respect for the cultural backgrounds of your students—is required when introducing professional norms for operating within U.S. organizations.

As you teach, be aware of the tensions in our discipline regarding how to accomplish educational goals such as developing our students' intellectual abilities. In our discussions (and debates) we ask, for instance, whether we should prioritize teaching theoretical concepts to students instead of concentrating on developing their application skills. Reflecting on these tensions will allow you to decide where you are situating your teaching philosophy in contrast to other viewpoints. Within our disciplines we often articulate the goals we desire for students. What is viewed as desirable knowledge influences what is contained in our textbooks, scholarly journals, and course curriculum—for instance, supporting our points of view with narratives that capture the *lived experience* of participants or placing greater emphasis on information that can be quantified. The educational system is not judgment-free; it is a political system which privileges some forms of knowledge over others.

Knowing some of the pedagogy and epistemology-based issues will allow you to intelligently reflect on decisions about how to teach your courses. Reviewing Sprague's (1993) guidelines for speech communication pedagogy will introduce you to larger issues associated with teaching—issues faced by all teachers who take their responsibilities seriously and who view learning as a life-long process.

Being aware of your strategy for gaining information may assist you in maximizing your chances of getting what you need to function effectively. With preparation, practice, creativity, and time, you will begin to see yourself attaining the characteristics of an artist. You will move beyond a focus on prescribed steps to creative interaction and, as a result, your confidence and talent will increase.

Cited Readings

Allen, R. R., & Rueter, T. (1990). *Teaching assistant strategies: An introduction to college teaching.* Dubuque, IO: Kendall-Hunt.

Burkel-Rothfuss, N. L., & Fink, D. S. (1993). Student perceptions of teaching assistants (TAs). *Basic Communication Course Annual, 5*, 71–100.

Darling, A. L., & Dewey, M. L. (1990). Teaching assistant socialization: Communication with peer leaders about teaching and learning. *Teaching and Teacher Education, 6,* 315–326.

Fuller, F. F. (1969). Concerns of teachers: A developmental conceptualization. *American Educational Research Journal, 6,* 207–226.

Fuller, F. F., & Parsons, J. S. (1972, April). *Current research on the concerns of teachers.* Paper presented at the meeting of the American Educational Research Association, Chicago, IL.

Galvin, K. M. (1990). Classroom roles of the teacher. In J. A. Daly, G. W. Friedrich, & A. L. Vangelisti (Eds.). *Teaching communication: Theory, research, and methods* (pp. 195–206). Hillsdale, NJ: Lawrence Erlbaum.

Gray, W. S. (1930). Survey of current methods in training prospective college teachers. in W. S. Gray (Ed.), *The training of college teachers: Including their preliminary preparation and in-service improvement* (pp. 80–90). Chicago: University of Chicago Press.

McKeachie, W. J. (1994). *Teaching tips: Strategies, research, and theory for college and university teachers* (9th ed.). Lexington, MA: D. C. Heath.

Menges, R. J. (1996). Experiences of newly hired faculty. In L. Richlin (Ed.), *To improve the academy* (Vol. 15, pp. 169–182). Stillwater, OK: New Forums Press.

Nadler, L. B. (1985, November). *The graduate teaching assistant: How much autonomy should be granted in the basic interpersonal communication course?* Paper presented at the meeting of the Speech Communication Association, Denver, CO.

Ryan, M. P., & Martens, G. G. (1989). *Planning a college course: A guidebook for the graduate teaching assistant.* Ann Arbor, MI: The University of Michigan, The National Center for Research to Improve Postsecondary Teaching and Learning (NCRIPTAL).

Sprague, J. (1990). The goals of communication education. In J. A. Daly, G. W. Friedrich, & A. L. Vangelisti (Eds.), *Teaching communication: Theory, research, and methods* (pp. 19–37). Hillsdale, NJ: Lawrence Erlbaum.

Sprague, J. (1993). Retrieving the research agenda for communication education: Asking the pedagogical questions that are "embarrassments to theory." *Communication Education, 42,* 106–122.

Staton, A. Q., & Darling, A. L. (1989). Socialization of teaching assistants. In J. D. Nyquist, R. D. Abbott, & D. H. Wulff (Eds.), *Teaching assistant training in the 1990s: Vol. 39. New directions for teaching and learning* (pp. 15–22). San Francisco: Jossey-Bass.

Staton-Spicer, A. Q., & Marty-White, C. R. (1981). A framework for instructional communication theory: The relationship between teacher communication concerns and classroom behavior. *Communication Education, 30,* 354–366.

Svinicki, M. (1995–96). A dozen reasons why we should prepare graduate students to teach. *The Journal of Graduate Teaching Assistant Development, 3,* 5–8.

Trank, D. M. (1990). Directing multiple sections of the basic course. In J. A. Daly, G. W. Friedrich, & A. L. Vangelisti (Eds.), *Teaching communication: Theory, research, and methods* (pp. 405–416). Hillsdale, NJ: Lawrence Erlbaum.

Willer, L. R. (1993). Are you a real teacher?: Student perceptions of the graduate student as instructor of the basic communication course. *Basic Communication Course Annual, 5,* 43–70.

Chapter 2
Surviving the First Week of Classes

Your first week of teaching will be stressful due to the dual responsibilities of being teacher and student. You will understandably be concerned about your performance in the graduate courses in which you are enrolled as well as the undergraduate courses you must teach. Thorough preparation and positive self talk are two factors which can significantly reduce, although not eliminate your anxiety. Your preparation can be conceptualized in two stages which include understanding (a) department expectations and (b) how to handle your first week in the classroom (see Hendrix, 1999 for further information).

Department Expectations

The first step in preparing to teach is to be aware of what you will teach, whether you will teach independently (for example, you are the teacher rather than assisting a professor), and who is responsible for developing the course syllabi and materials. As a result, it is important for you to contact your basic course director to obtain answers to these questions. Inquire whether your department and campus offer an orientation session for new graduate teaching assistants. If orientations are offered, be sure to attend. Whether you are attending an orientation session or meeting directly with your basic course director, you need to know:

- o How the department conceptualizes the course and its importance to the rest of the curriculum and the discipline.
- o Why the course is structured as it is (or what material you are required to cover if you are responsible for designing the course).
- o How do the instructional units within the class fit together? For example, how should you make transitions from one set of concepts to another?
- o What is the big picture? For instance, why are papers required in a small group discussion class?
- o What are your administrative responsibilities?
- o Can you add or drop students? If yes, what is the procedure and an acceptable circumstance? If no, who has the authority to do so?
- o Are students who add the course after the first week allowed to make-up assignments?

- How many office hours are required? Are they required on different days of the week?
- What accommodations can and should be made for disabled students?
- What kind of assistance with your teaching will be provided by the basic course director? Is it appropriate to contact your basic course director at home?
- Is there a lead GTA available for consultation?
- Will the basic course director or lead GTA be available to observe your practice of your first lecture, discussion, or small group facilitation?
- Are you required to use a standard syllabus, set of assignments, or series of exams? (Chapter 3 addresses syllabus construction.)

In some cases, you will know in advance what you will be expected to teach and how many sections per term. However, some institutions may not make your assignment until a week prior to the onset of the term. While this is not ideal, you can still engage in some preliminary preparation by asking which courses you might be asked to teach and developing lessons for the first few weeks in the term for each course. Your preparation will not be a waste of time as you (a) may be assigned to the other course at some other time during your assistantship and (b) should be able to explain the connection among the courses in your discipline to your students.

Emphasizing the First Week of Teaching

Following the guidelines noted above, you will have a macro-level idea of the course and your responsibilities. It is also advisable to consider specifically how you will handle yourself during the first week of the term as you attempt to build your credibility in your own mind and in the eyes of your students. You should consider preparing for the first week, teaching the first class period, and what to do after teaching your first class.

Preparing for the first week. Your self-concerns can be mitigated, to a certain degree, by preparation and positive self-talk. Positive self-talk is possible when you can tell yourself you are thoroughly prepared. In addition to lesson planning, you may choose to begin this process of confidence building by confronting your worst fears. Two major steps to confidence-building include identifying your fears, then working to alleviate the possibility of the fear scenario playing out.

Ask yourself what is it you are most afraid of happening in your classroom? That you will not know the material? That your students will talk continuously as you review the syllabus? That someone will ask if you are a student and question your qualifications to teach? After determining what you fear, ask what aspect of the anxiety-producing situation is under your control. For example, if you fear you will not know the material, prepare in advance and confirm the accuracy of your interpretation of the content and examples with your basic course director or more experienced peer. If you fear students will talk continuously, plan to introduce yourself and request that students not talk as you take roll and learn names (see also Chapter 8 on discipline and motivation). Finally, if you fear your knowledge will be questioned, remember that you are a graduate student who was competitively selected to teach this undergraduate course. Remember your extensive review of the material and consider how you can communicate your preparation in a non-defensive manner. As you begin class, mention that you are a graduate student and note your special interests within the discipline along with the fact that you are looking forward to sharing your excitement and knowledge of the material. For every fear, determine how you can reduce the possibility of it materializing. Be realistic and address only the aspects of the potential problem within your control.

So far in Chapter 2, I have discussed:

o   Knowing your syllabus (whether you create it or it is a standard one required of all GTAs).
o   Knowing your course content and how the units connect with one another throughout the term.
o   Knowing your coordinator's expectations.
o   Knowing department and campus policies.

Yet there are a number of additional considerations, which include:

o   Visiting your classroom in advance.
o   Visualizing yourself in the room.
o   Practicing out loud.
o   Dressing appropriately.
o   Deciding how you wish to be addressed.
o   Consciously acknowledging characteristics which may influence interaction with your students (for example, race, gender, age).

Once you know what you will be teaching, also determine where you will be teaching and visit the site. Check for supplies (for example, chalk) and needed equipment (for example, VCR and monitor). Do you need a podium for your students? Do you need a desk at the front of the room for your handouts and books? Do you prefer a standing or desktop podium? Consider the kinds of seating. Are you scheduled to teach small group discussion in a room which has student seats bolted to the floor? If what you need is not there (or the room is not appropriate for the type of class you are teaching), make requests immediately in order to determine if your needs can be met or if you must work with whatever is currently in the classroom.

After you know how your classroom looks, visualize yourself teaching in the room. Visualize how you will enter the classroom, where you will put your materials, and how you will use the blackboard. Visualize yourself as you move from behind the podium and closer to your students. Ideally, you will have time to do more than just visualize your behavior. Hopefully, you will have time to enter the room and actually practice the first 30 minutes of what you plan to say during the first class period. Practice out loud; not in your head. This is particularly important if you will not have microteaching (practice teaching) during your departmental orientation. At the very least, arrive at your assigned room early so you can follow the guidelines noted above. If there are major shortcomings, you will not have time to request changes.

Do not let the first day of class actually be the first time you hear yourself reviewing the syllabus, starting to lecture, and introducing yourself. If you do not have access to your classroom, practice your entire first class period out loud while audio or video recording your teaching. Listen to yourself, assess your strengths, weaknesses, and the time it takes to get through the material. Make adjustments and practice again.

You are functioning within a variety of departmental and institutional contexts. One strategy for building credibility involves dressing more professionally in the classroom. You will only be a year or two older than some of your students and others may be two decades (or more) older than you. Dressing professionally is one way to communicate that you are the assigned instructor and that you take your responsibilities seriously. When you are a fairly young GTA, your dress is one factor which can assist you in creating an element of distinction between you and undergraduates who are close to your age. Your dress can also communicate to older students that you are serious and that they will need to interact with you as their instructor rather than a *young adult* who might remind them of a son, daughter, or grandchild. What is appropriate dress (a suit might be too much) will be determined by the formality or informality of your surroundings. What you wear may also change somewhat after you have established some degree of credibility and you are approaching the mid-to-latter part of the term. Even in the case of informal departments, during the initial weeks of the term, I strongly suggest a dress shirt and nice pants (for example, khakis) for young men and a dressier look (for example, skirt and blouse, dress, dress slacks and blouse) for young women. Your students are assessing how you look as well as what you say to determine your credibility and command of the class. They are also assessing your knowledge.

Your class needs to know how you want to be addressed. Do you want to be called "Yunlai," "Ms. Bulusu," "Mrs. Thompson," and so forth. Until you have earned your doctoral degree, it is quite inappropriate to have your students refer to you as "professor" or "doctor." Consider the possibilities in advance. Your final decision may actually be determined once you are in class and you see who is enrolled. For example, if most of your students are the same age as you, you may decide you want to be addressed as "Ms. Bell" to, along with your dress, assist you in creating the image of *instructor* in the minds of your students. On the other hand, if many of your students are your parents' age, you may feel uncomfortable asking them to refer to you as "Mr. Skidmore." As a result, as they refer to you as "David," you may want to rely on your dress and clear grading policies to assist you in establishing your role as *teacher.*

Before entering your classroom on the first day, it is imperative that you consider how you interact with people who come from backgrounds or gender different from your own. What are some of the images you hold of members of other groups including positive and negative traits? How do you plan to interact with members of these groups in your classroom? If you hold extremely positive or negative feelings (or even ambivalent ones), what will you do to mitigate those feelings to ensure you are being as fair as possible to your students? Above all else, try to get to know your students as individuals. Do not overlook group membership (for example, saying you are colorblind can be quite offensive) but also seek to know the individual. Expand your horizons by reading about people whose life experiences are different from your own. Also make a point of interacting with a diverse groups of people. The process is not an easy one but is imperative that you expand your knowledge of not only disciplinary content but people. The United States is becoming increasing diverse. You must learn perspectives besides the one you were raised with as a child. Doing so requires self-reflection and interaction with people who are different (in some ways) from yourself.

When the big day arrives, you will definitely be nervous. Follow the same recommendations you will make to your students (see Chapter 7) for reducing communication anxiety.

Beginning the first day of class. Decide whether you will enter the classroom to begin class, or whether you want to already be in the room at the front of class as students arrive. In the latter case, what will you doing as your students arrive? When it is time for class:

- o   Identify yourself.
- o   Indicate how you want to be addressed.
- o   Identify the course and section number.
- o   Give students time to leave if they are in the wrong room.
- o   Be prepared for students arriving late on the first day. (Be patient.)
- o   Build your credibility by briefly sharing your background and capabilities with your students.
- o   To assist in building a credible image, demonstrate organization and general preparedness.
- o   Explain the course content and relevance to the students who are enrolled.
- o   Review the syllabus.
- o   Explain that changes may occur and you will give as much notice as possible.
- o   Take time to answer questions (count to 10 to give an opportunity for them to think).
- o   Take roll.
- o   Practice student names before going to class, then ask if students want to be called something other than their formal names. Where necessary, ask for assistance with pronunciation. Do not abbreviate names or assign American names to international students. Do not change the names of any students (native or non-native) whose names are difficult to pronounce. Learn to pronounce them properly. Do not fall victim to the prejudiced view that all members of particular groups look alike. They do not. Only identical twins look alike. Identify each student's distinguishing features, and learn their names.
- o   Begin teaching your scheduled lesson for the day or conducting exercises.
- o   Make time for questions.
- o   If you release your class early, explain the rationale for doing so. Failure to provide an explanation may communicate disinterest, lack of preparedness, and so on.
- o   Take roll again before ending class.
- o   Stay after class for a few moments. Failure to do so may communicate that you are not approachable. Give shy students a chance to interact with you.

You will be quite relieved after finishing the teaching in your first class. Find a private place and praise yourself. After complimenting yourself, some reflection is now in order.

After class ends. Review your schedule for the remainder of the day. If you have another course to teach, sit for a moment and review how you want to handle the next class period. Consider any necessary adaptations to how you handled yourself in the first class and decide how to implement any changes. Then go in and teach your second class while remembering that this is a completely new group of students. Keep your enthusiasm level high and do not take shortcuts. Remember that the second group of students will be hearing your introduction to the course for the first time.

After you have finished your teaching for the day, make time to sit and assess what went well and what could be improved. Write this in your journal (see Chapter 10) so you can make those adaptations for the next term. Consider what changes need to be made immediately, as well as what you should continue in your approach to the next scheduled class period. Decide when you will prepare or review your content for the next class period. Check in with your basic course director and review your accomplishments. During the discussion be sure to mention what you handled well and what you enjoyed the most. Finally, do not forget about preparing for and attending your own graduate courses!

Cited Readings

Hendrix, K. G. (1999). Constructing an orientation session to address graduate teaching assistant (GTA) self concerns. *Journal of Graduate Teaching Assistant Development, 6,* 65–72.

Chapter 3
Designing a Syllabus

If your department allows you to create your own syllabus, take the responsibility seriously. Your students need enough information to determine the (a) content of the course, (b) administrative policies, (c) type of assignments, and (d) grading system.

You may be fortunate enough to have syllabi from other GTAs and professors readily available for your review. If this is the case, you can use those syllabi as a guide. Copying someone else's syllabi verbatim may present significant problems for you and your students if you do not carefully review the information to ensure that you agree with the reading sequence, the nature of the assignments, and the grading system. If you do not agree, or you are experiencing difficulty determining why the course has been structured in a particular way, inquire regarding the rationale for the course design. If the author of the syllabus cannot address your questions regarding the reasoning behind the class structure, create your own.

In order to provide the required level of detail, you cannot simply prepare your lessons on a weekly basis. Think through the entire course and the logical presentation of the content units. *Thinking through the entire course* means to read all of the material you are assigning your students to determine which chapters should be presented together, in what order, and when in the term. Ideally, you will have several months to prepare for the course you are teaching. Under less than ideal circumstances, and when adopting another person's syllabus is not feasible, quickly review the reading materials and assign your chapters in a reasonable manner. For example, prepare to explain to your students why they are reading Chapter 2 before Chapter 1, and so on. Do not blindly follow the recommendations in the instructor's manual unless the recommended format makes sense to you. (An instructor's manual is available, upon request, from Wadsworth or your textbook representative.) One advantage of instructors' manuals is the provision of an idea of the order in which to teach the chapters on both a semester and quarter system. Keep in mind that you can assign students to do some reading on their own even when you do not plan to formally cover the content in class.

Syllabi typically follow a format similar to the following:

Instructor Name   Semester

Contact Information   Department

Course Name and Number

Section Number

- o Course Description
- o Attendance Policy
- o Disabled Student Assistance
- o Special Department Expectations, for example
    - o Attendance at speaking colloquiums.
    - o Participation in experiments
- o Grading System
- o Overview of Major Assignments
- o Daily Class Schedule, for example:
    - o Assigned readings
    - o Due dates for assignments
    - o Exam and quiz dates
    - o Speaking days
- o Holidays, Add/Drop Deadlines, Conferences
- o Final Examination Date/Time
- o Student Resources

Your syllabus should not be two pages in length nor should it be ten pages. Your students need a clear picture of the course but they should not become confused due to unnecessary detail. If time allows, create a draft of your syllabus for review by your basic course director. Be sure your syllabus is neat, legible, and free of typographical errors. This document also provides students with information about you and your capabilities. Have extra copies of the syllabus for students who add during the first day of class.

Each section of your syllabus requires attention to detail as follows:

Identifying Information

List your name as you wish to be addressed. For example, you might type "Orin Johnson" or "Mr. O. Johnson" on your syllabus in anticipation of how you will introduce yourself to your students. Decide whether you will give them your home telephone number. If you are uncomfortable listing your home number, your e-mail address is a viable option. Do not assume your students have computers at home. Make certain they are familiar with e-mail and how to reach your mailbox using campus computers. Include your office hours by noting the days and times you are available. Also indicate that you are available by appointment made in advance. In the case of multiple section courses, list your specific section number, meeting days, and class time.

Course Description

Develop a class description which is one or two paragraphs in length. In your description mention the goals and objectives of the course and what students can expect to learn and incorporate in their daily lives. Also list any course prerequisites or recommended courses which should succeed your class.

Policies

Your syllabus should include a statement regarding excused and unexcused absences. Do not makeup a policy-be sure to obtain approval from your basic course director to avoid legal problems. Make a statement regarding your willingness to assist students with visible and invisible disabilities. Investigate the services which are available on your campus and what you are reasonably expected to do for student who need this assistance before forming your statement. Also note any special department expectations—for example, attendance at colloquia. If your department expects students to participate in experiments or to attend colloquia or public forums, you should indicate:

- o Where students can find information about the various events.
- o How many are required.
- o How grades will be affected.
- o Any deadlines for compliance.
- o Be clear regarding the punishment for plagiarism and cheating.

Grading System

Your students are entitled to know how many assignments are in the course, the nature of those assignments, and their relative weight. They also need an idea of when the graded assignments are due. You should not be teaching your class on a week-to-week (or day-to-day) basis without having the entire course mapped out for your students as well as yourself. Also inform your students of the percentage required to earn a particular final grade-for instance, is a B- a score of 80% or 83%? Do not assume they innately understand your grading scale.

Daily Class Schedule and Assignment Overview

A daily schedule lists the reading assignments for each class period and should also note any assignments which might be due on a particular date. Student papers, for example, might be due on the same day you will be discussing Chapters 10–12 in a particular text. Providing due dates (with an understanding that you may need to make some changes) allows your students to coordinate their studying and workload across all of their courses-in other words, this information helps them plan how to effectively use their time.

Your daily schedule should also list important dates such as the last day to add or drop a course, school holidays, and day when you will be out of town (for example, attending a conference). You should also list the exact date, time, and location of your final examination. At some institutions, students take finals on a completely different schedule than the rest of the term. Be sure your students are aware of their final date and highlight this information on your syllabus. Including the date and time of graduation is usually encouraging and even exciting for those who are about to complete their studies.

Assignment overviews typically are one paragraph descriptions of the major assignments. You might, for instance, describe two student essays by indicating the concept or phenomenon to be researched and discussed by students. You might also note how many pages are required, the minimum number of citations, and the desired citation system. In the case of oral presentations, you would inform students of the type of speech (or small group format), time limits, minimum number of citations, acceptable topics, and so forth.

Student Resources

To further benefit your students, you might choose to list campus resources which are available to them. Your list should include services such as tutoring in English, assistance with test anxiety, and speaking laboratories. You may also want to include student psychological and health services.

Remember your syllabus is a visual roadmap for you and your students. At any given time, your syllabus should provide a macro-and micro-level view of your course. The syllabus should be concise enough that students can glance through and see the big picture yet detailed enough that they can determine exactly what will be covered the during the following week.

Chapter 4
Knowing Yourself as Classroom Teacher

In your basic undergraduate education in the Communication discipline, you learned that our perception of the world influences how we interact with others as well as how we approach particular situations. You also learned that perception is a culturally embedded view of the world which is learned by observing the verbal and nonverbal messages around us. We learn what is expected of us in our talk and our behavior as members of a particular speech community. Each of us belongs to several co-cultures (for example, Black, female, and adolescent) which allows people from diverse backgrounds to find some areas of common ground. However, intercultural studies confirm that we often focus primarily on how another person differs from us rather than what we have in common. As we focus on what is different, we may rely on what we have heard about members of that particular group (having had only limited interaction) and stereotypical images generated by mediated messages—for example, television, magazines, and movies. As an instructor, you will interact with people from different backgrounds. To maximize your effectiveness, you should face your biases, recognize yourself as a GTA of color (if applicable), and consider the context of your teaching.

Facing Learned Biases

As we enter the classroom to teach others it is imperative that we teach the entire class and that we do so as fairly as we can. Preparing your content is crucial but is not sufficient; you must also compose a mind open to students from cultural groups which are different from your own. According to Dodd, "culture is the holistic interrelationship of a group's identity, beliefs, values, activities, rules, customs, communication patterns, and institutions" (1998, p. 36). In order to create an in-group cultural identity, group members must distinguish themselves from others; thus, creating an out-group. One danger associated with group solidarity is the presence of an ethnocentric perspective. Ethnocentrism means that members of a particular group believe that they are superior to others. As a teacher, you must assess your cultural expectations and biases and you must be prepared to address those of your students as they interact with you and their peers.

First, you must know yourself as a person and how who you are may affect your interactions with your students. Calloway-Thomas, Cooper, & Blake (1999) state:

As human beings, we are essentially wrapped up within our peculiar cultural milieu. Hence, we are anchored in that milieu and we need to know that culture well before we can attempt to know or understand others coming from different cultural milieu . . . Knowledge of why people are the way they are is central to effective intercultural communication. (pp. 41–42)

Consider creating a self-concept composite, where you list your characteristics (for example, loyal, friendly, brother, and so on). While the list will not be perfect because no list can completely capture your humanity, ask yourself whether the 10 characteristics represent you fairly well. Do you like what you see? Do people from other backgrounds tend to like what they see? Getting along with one person from a particular culture does not automatically equate to your ability to interact with other members of that group. Also, as you assess the nature of your relationships with associates from diverse backgrounds, are you basing you judgment solely on your perceptions, or have you received confirmation from others? Do not fall victim to the belief that you know or can say X "because some of my best friends are Y."

Even if your campus is homogeneous, we live in a diverse world. Read and expose yourself to other perspectives.

As an instructor, why not vary the images and writings you use? Instead of teaching primarily using speeches and writings by White male and female speakers, incorporate speeches by Hispanic, Asian, Native, African-American and international speakers. If you cannot readily locate video-tapes, allow your students to work with written copies of speeches. Move beyond the obvious traditional speeches (for example, "I Have a Dream") and expand your students' knowledge of great but perhaps lesser known speeches.

Do some research on the importance of small group interaction in collectivist cultures. Learn about leadership characteristics and responsibilities in such cultures. Share this information with your students. Compare and contrast how group interaction is approached in collectivist versus individualistic cultures.

Be sure that you are allowing all voices to be heard in your class. And do not simply call on students of color (or a White student attending a historically Black institution) only when the topic deals with some aspect of what you perceive to be their culture. Make a point of motivating all of your students to participate in general class discussion. Build a safe, respectful environment for people to speak and one where you build their confidence and self-esteem.

In turn, you will be able to assist your students and peers in expanding their knowledge, understanding, and appreciation of other groups, lifestyles, and world views. More importantly, know yourself and never lose sight of your students as unique individuals.

Interpersonal relationships. As stated earlier, learning about yourself is the first step to preparing yourself to develop relationships with your students. Traditionally, interpersonal communication is conceptualized as perceiving a relationship as a positive one where, over time, both parties choose to continue to relate to each other (Galvin & Wilkinson, 1996). However, Stewart and Logan (1998) mention that any interaction which involves seeing another's personal characteristics is an interpersonal moment (as opposed social or culturally-based motivated interaction). Therefore, Stewart believes that classroom interactions can be interpersonal even though you will only be with your students for a short period (one term) and you will be interacting primarily in the social role of teacher.

When discussing interpersonal dimensions of classroom teaching, Lowman (1995) discusses several strategies which may assist instructors in developing interpersonal skills with their students. These strategies include:

o Learning student names-and other relevant data (which they perceive you should know).
o Arriving to class 5–10 minutes early in order to speak to students informally.
o Posting and announcing your office hours.
o Showing an interest in your students—for example, attending a play in which one of your students is acting.
o Giving some degree of personal freedom by making suggestions rather than directives, providing rational justification for assignments, giving students choices, and allowing students more independence on projects as the semester progresses.

I would add to this list, if you do not already possess them, develop a sense of humor and patience. You do not need to disclose high levels of personal information, however, if you want your students to disclose so you can get to know them, the process should be a reciprocal one.

Interpersonal communication maximizes the personal. You acknowledge that the individuals you are addressing are students but you also recognize their uniqueness and, in some cases, their needs as people. Being closed to revealing yourself to your students does not promote an interpersonal environment.

Fairness and ethical behavior. As you begin to recognize the members of your class as more than members of particular co-cultures including that of *students,* another issue will arise-that of fairness. Because we are human and we do have preferences, we will be attracted to some students more than others. As I have mentioned earlier, our perception will influence our interaction. So we must be careful not to engage in more conversation with students we like, give them longer periods to voice their opinion, provide them with more positive nonverbal and verbal feedback, and so on. I am afraid there is no simple solution except to be aware of how we handle ourselves (see Chapter 10) in the classroom and to make adjustments in our behavior as needed.

Showing favoritism to particular students during class discussion is a problem but the matter may be exacerbated if you do so when grading. Every opportunity should be used to engage in *blind* grading. If your students are submitting essays or some other written assignment, have them use their student identification numbers rather than their names. On longer assignments, an alternative would be to have students put their names on a separate page at the end of the document. The students could write *end of report* at the bottom of their last page of text, thereby, signaling that you should grade the paper before turning to the final identification page.

Attribution theory informs us that we will locate external reasons to account for poor or inappropriate performance by ourselves or people we like. (For example: *"My roommates were so noisy I could not concentrate."*) On the other hand, the locus for those we do not like will be internally defined, that is, seen as a flaw in that person's character or make-up. (We might think, for example, *not very bright, lazy,* and so forth). These attributions will manifest themselves in how we interact with these students. Give yourself every opportunity to fairly assess the performance of each student whether you like or dislike them. When in doubt, remove the student's name (and your comments) and ask the basic course director or an experienced peer to score the paper.

In addition to grading, do not make exceptions to your stated classroom policies for students you like more than others. As a checkpoint, ask if you would do the same for any student in that same circumstance. If not, the matter requires further reflection and consultation with your basic course director before a final decision is made.

Graduate Teaching Assistants of Color

Although the numbers of faculty of color (for example, African, Asian, Hispanic, and Native-American) are increasing, you may find yourself as part of a small percentage of faculty teaching in a predominantly White institution. How you are received by your students will depend on their upbringing including their exposure (and the nature of that exposure) to individuals like you. Just as international students (see Chapter 5) must acknowledge who they are and the fact that students may focus on differences, the same is true for you.

In some of my research (Hendrix, 1994, 1997, 1998), participants indicate that preparedness is important for both Black and White professors but more information is desired about the credentials, research, and professional experience of the Black professors. Be aware that while all GTAs have a difficult time establishing their credibility, given your status as a person of color, your task may be greater than that of your peers. If you feel comfortable enough, introduce the matter to your basic course director and seek advice. Your basic course director may need some guidance regarding how you want to be treated and whether you would be offended if issues such as race and gender are a regular part of teaching assistant seminar discussions. Whether you are offended or not, I recommend that you review some of the literature about racial identity development and share this information with your basic course director.

Find a mentor who will *not* address your teaching from a *color-blind* perspective. While there are people who cannot distinguish various shades of blue or brown, no one with sight is color-blind to race when our physical phenotypes match the characteristics of particular group membership (whether accurate or not). Who you are, including your race and skin color, will impact the dynamics of your classroom. To grow as a classroom instructor, you need a mentor who will acknowledge every aspect of who you are rather than overlooking certain characteristics.

Remember to:

Be yourself. Regardless of your co-cultures, and even if you have a twin, you are your own person. Let your personality surface and do not create a false personality for your class.

Be prepared. Know your material and also anticipate how you will address challenges which may occur from particular students in your class.

Be confident. In part, confidence is derived from knowing you are prepared and comfortable with yourself as a person and teacher. Also, remember that you have been competitively-selected as a department teaching assistant.

Enjoy your opportunity to teach. View your assistantship as an opportunity to expand your skills and to gain first hand knowledge of the teaching experience. This knowledge will assist you in deciding whether you want to enter the professoriate as a career.

Do not stereotype your class as antagonistic. Learn about each one of your students; create a relationship with each (willing) student.

Consider other possible reasons for negative student response. At the same time, do not believe you must deny the possibility that your race, ethnicity, or skin color are influencing the classroom and one-to-one dynamics.

Introduce bias as one of several possible motivations for student misbehavior. When speaking to your student privately, get the issue of bias on the table and address it professionally. For instance, you might tell a student your perception is that the student is biased against your ethnicity or race. You can say there is nothing you can do to undo what the student has learned over a number of years but you are the instructor and, as a result, expect respectful treatment. You can outline what you find to be acceptable ways to ask a question, appeal a grade, and so forth.

Do not to allow a negative situation to detrimentally impact all relationships. One or two students may be creating a problem for you rather than your entire class. Continue to show respect for your students while, justifiably, expecting respect in return.

(Note: White GTAs may benefit from reviewing this particular set of recommendations, if you are teaching at historically Black colleges and universities (HBCUs) or other campuses where you will have a high percentage of students of color enrolled in your courses.)

Regardless of your demographic characteristics and co-cultural memberships, once you have a grasp on who you are as a person and the sources influencing your development, you will be better equipped to interact with your students. This is particularly true if you are willing to assess what biases must be held in check as you enter the classroom and interaction with your students during office hours. We all have biases. Acknowledge your biases, then actively engage in what Weinstein and Obear (1992) refer to as the lifelong process of "unlearning" those negative, unproductive beliefs.

Learn how to develop relationships based on fact rather than fiction and stereotypes.

The Context of Your Teaching

Lastly, in conjunction with assessing who you are, closely observe your surroundings and the corresponding cultural contexts in your department, campus, and community. Consistent with this perspective, McKeachie (1994, p. 5) notes that GTAs should determine the role of a faculty member not only in their department but at their institution because "a course cannot be divorced from the total college or university culture." Familiarize yourself with your surroundings on at least, three levels—departmental, campus, and community.

Department. Within your department, inquire about the following:
- o What students typically enroll in your course—freshmen, seniors, returning adults?
- o Why do students take the course? Is it required for their major, for graduation, or is it an elective?
- o Where do GTAs fit into the department faculty?
- o What contributions to the department are expected of GTAs?

Campus. Your campus has a personality of its own and a certain type of relationship—either interconnected with the community or set apart. You should know:
- o Whether the campus faculty value interaction with community groups and organizations.
- o If it is a commuter campus where students are there primarily to attend classes.
- o Whether you can expect frequent interaction with your students.
- o If it is reasonable to design assignments which require students to meet on campus.
- o Whether you will be expected to teach off-campus.

Community. As you prepare for class, whether you will be teaching on- or off campus, you need to have a sense of the community in which you teach. Most of the students entering your classroom have grown up and attended schools within that same area. As you plan your course lessons and develop your grading criteria, it is beneficial for you to know:
- o If the language is different from where you grew up.
- o How members of the community perceive appropriate interaction.

- o   What resources are available to you in the community—for example, guest speakers, facilities, and so on.
- o   The literacy and poverty rate.
- o   If the school system adequately prepares students for post-secondary learning?
- o   The relationship between local community colleges and your college or university.

If you are new to the community, this information may not be readily available. Do not be afraid to ask questions. Weinstein and Obear (1992) note that fear is dangerous as it immobilizes its victims. Raimy (1975) says that fear is based on a series of misconceptions about (a) the harmfulness of the feared situation, (b) the likelihood of being disintegrated by the situation, and (c) one's ability to change the fearful reaction. Ask questions and make observations (keep them tentative) in order to reduce your anxiety of the unknown. Speak to your basic course director, department chair, and other graduate students and GTAs to increase your understanding of the environments in which you will live, study, and teach.

Assessing the character of your department, campus, and community provides valuable information regarding the expected norms for your behavior and that of your students and peers. You may then make decisions regarding whether and how much to adapt your behavior to meet the expectations of the various cultural communities within which you will live and interact. Gaining knowledge and reducing bias is a lifelong process of expanding our experiences and understanding, while unlearning inaccurate beliefs.

Cited Readings

Calloway-Thomas, C., Cooper, P. J., & Blake, C. (1999). *Intercultural communication: Roots and routes.* Boston: Allyn and Bacon.

Dodd, D. H. (1998). *Dynamics of intercultural communication.* Boston: McGraw-Hill.

Galvin, K. M., & Wilkinson, C. A. (1996). The communication process: Impersonal and interpersonal. In K. M. Galvin, & P. Cooper (Eds.), *Making connections: Readings in relational communication* (pp. 4–10). Los Angeles: Roxbury.

Hendrix, K. G. (1994). *Is the classroom really like, To Sir, With Love?: Six case studies of professor credibility and race.* Unpublished doctoral dissertation, University of Washington, Seattle.

Hendrix, K. G. (1997). Student perceptions of verbal and nonverbal communication cues leading to images of professor credibility. *The Howard Journal of Communication, 8,* 251–274.

Hendrix, K. G. (1998). Student perceptions of the influence of race on professor credibility. *Journal of Black Studies, 28,* 738–763.

Lowman, J. (1995). *Mastering the techniques of teaching* (2nd ed.). San Francisco: Jossey-Bass.

McKeachie, W. J. (1994). Teaching tips: Strategies, research, and theory for college and university teachers (9th ed.). Lexington, MA: D. C. Heath.

Raimy, V. (1975). *Misunderstandings of the self: Cognitive psychotherapy and the misconception hypothesis.* San Francisco: Jossey-Bass.

Stewart, J., & Logan, C. (1998). *Together: Communicating interpersonally.* Boston: McGraw-Hill.

Weinstein, G., & Obear, K. (1992). Bias issues in the classroom: Encounters with the teaching self. In M. Adams (Ed.), *Promoting diversity in college classrooms: Innovative responses for the curriculum, faculty, and institutions* (39–50). San Francisco: Jossey-Bass.

Recommended Readings

Cross, W. E., Jr. (1991). *Shades of black: Diversity in African-American identity.* Philadelphia: Temple University Press.

Eschbach, K., & Gomez, C. (1998). Choosing Hispanic identity: Ethnic identity switching among respondents to high school and beyond. *Social Science Quarterly, 79,* 74–90.

Ford-Ahmed, T., & Orbe, M. (1994, November). *Bodies bonded by temporality: Surviving ethnic prejudice in a majority host institution.* Paper presented at the meeting of the Speech Communication Association, New Orleans, LA.

Gonzalez, A., Houston, M., & Chen, V. (1997). *Our voices: Essays in culture, ethnicity, and communication* (2nd ed.). Los Angeles: Roxbury.

Gudykunst, W. B., Newmark, E., & Asante, M. K. (1994). *Handbook of international and intercultural communication.* Thousand Oaks, CA: Sage.

Hamlet, J. (1992, November). *Sister-to-sister: Conversations with African-American women in academia.* Paper presented at the meeting of the Speech Communication Association, Chicago, IL.

Hardiman, R., & Jackson, B. W. (1992). Racial identity development: Understanding racial dynamics in college classrooms and on campus. In M. Adams, (Ed.)., *Promoting diversity in college classrooms: Innovative responses for the curriculum, faculty, and institutions* (pp. 21–37). San Francisco: Jossey-Bass.

Ibrahim, F., Ohnishi, H., & Sandhu, D. S. (1997). Asian American identity development: A culture specific model for south Asian Americans. *Journal of Multicultural Counseling and Development, 25,* 34–50.

Keith-Spiegel, P., Wittig, A. F., Perkins, D. V., Balogh, D. W., & Whitley, Jr., B. E. (1994). *The ethics of teaching: A casebook.* Muncie, IN: Ball State University.

Ladson-Billings, G. (1994). *The dreamkeepers: Successful teachers of African-American children.* San Francisco: Jossey-Bass.

Lee, W. S. (1998). In the names of Chinese women. *Quarterly Journal of Speech, 84,* 283–302.

Quigley, B. L., Nyquist, J., & Hendrix, K. G. (1993). Using videotape to promote teaching diversity in the classroom. In K. Lewis (Ed.), *3rd National Conference Proceedings on the Training and Employment of Graduate Teaching Assistants* (pp. 278–284). Stillwater, OK: New Forum Press.

Rubin, R. B., & Yoder, J. (1985). Ethical issues in the evaluation of communication behavior. *Communication Education, 34,* 13–17.

Staton, A. Q. (1990). An ecological perspective on college/university teaching. In J. A. Daly, G. W. Friedrich, & A. L. Vangelisti (Eds.), *Teaching communication: Theory, research, and methods* (pp. 39–52). Hillsdale, NJ: Lawrence Erlbaum.

Torres, V., & Phelps, R. E. (1997). *Hispanic American acculturation and ethnic identity: A bicultural model.* College Student Affairs Journal, 17, 53–68.

Wander, P. C., Martin, J. N., Nakayama, T. K. (1999). Whiteness and beyond: Socio-historical foundations of whiteness and contemporary challenges. In T. K. Nakayama & Martin, J. N. (Eds.), *Whiteness: The communication of social identity* (pp. 13–26). Thousand Oaks, CA: Sage.

Chapter 5
Strategies for Non-Native English Speaking GTAs

You should be aware that your students may perceive you differently than your American counterparts who are also graduate teaching assistants. Your students will be aware of your external characteristics such as race and gender. They will also pay attention to your dialect, accent, ethnicity, and nationality. While your students might have a heightened sense of the differences between you and themselves, it is still possible to identify areas of similarity and to create an environment where diversity can be appreciated.

Even if English is your first language, it is unrealistic to believe you completely present yourself with American mannerisms. It is not necessary for you to assimilate American ways. You may, however, need to make some adaptations in your presentation of material and your perceptions of appropriate classroom interaction. Your students will primarily be concerned that you are knowledgeable, comprehensible, and fair in your grading.

As a result, the following suggestions are offered to assist you in improving your teaching:

Before Classes Begin

- o Be sure you understand the material your department expects you to teach.
- o Clarify any questions you have about the course syllabus.
- o Recognize that American students ask questions and interrupt their instructors. Be prepared to answer immediately or to indicate that you will answer questions at another point during the class period or even during an office hour.
- o Try to familiarize yourself with American examples by listening to radio and watching television programs which are likely to be popular among your students.
- o Practice what you will say the first day of class out loud. If possible, audio record and listen to yourself and make any necessary adjustments. Ideally you should practice in front of an American listener and ask for feedback.
- o Take time to consider your images of American students in general and particular racial groups. Be careful not to assume the media images of particular groups (for example, African, Asian, Hispanic, or Native-Americans) are accurate. Be com-

mitted to getting to know each student as an individual rather than relying on stereotypes.

First Week of Classes

During the first week of classes briefly provide your students with information about you and your program of study at your institution.

Briefly discuss your view of teaching. State your responsibilities (for example, keeping office hours, providing assistance via e-mail) and the expectations you have of your students.

Tell your students you are open to them asking you to slow down or to repeat information. Let them know if they don't understand it is okay to politely inform you.

During Class

- o   Be prepared. Know your class material.
- o   Provide students with an overview of the day's class period and connect the content to previous or future classes.
- o   Remind students that you are available to assist them during office hours and make sure that you are indeed available.
- o   Use written material to assist your students in following your oral communication—for example, overhead projector, blackboard, handouts, or power point pages.
- o   Try to incorporate American examples and also include examples of how the concepts would be perceived in your country.
- o   If you do not understand what your students are saying, ask them. You can ask them the meaning of the joke or slang. You can even ask them to paraphrase their statement.
- o   Try to enjoy your interaction with your students and remind them of the benefits of having students (including yourself) from diverse backgrounds in the same course.

Other Information

Realize your students may see conflict differently. If you are worried about a student's complaint, ask one of your colleagues or your basic course director to sit in on the meeting between you and your student. Ask them to allow you to handle the interaction but to give you feedback after the meeting is over.

Ask your basic course director to observe you at least twice during the term. After the first visit, incorporate their advice. You can then obtain information about your improvement by having your director visit a second time.

If you want to keep your efforts to improve your teaching private, contact your campus teaching center and ask for confidential consultation. However, ideally, you will try to build a trusting relationship between you and your basic course director which will allow you to ask for advice and assistance.

Also refer to the self-assessment section of this guide (see Chapter 10) for more suggestions regarding strategies for evaluating your teaching.

Recommended Readings

Dale, P., & Wolf, J. C. (1988). *Speech communication for international students*. Englewood Cliffs, NJ: Prentice-Hall.

Hendrix, K. G. (in press). Assessment and skill development for ESL students in mainstream communication classes requiring oral presentations. *The Journal of the Association for Communication Administrators*.

Porter, P. A., & Grant, M. (1992). *Communicating effectively in English: Oral communication for non-native speakers* (2nd edition). Boston: Heinle and Heinle.

Quigley, B . L ., Hendrix, K. G., & Friesem, K. (1998). Graduate teaching assistant training: Preparing instructors to assist ESL students in the introductory public speaking course. *Basic Communication Course Annual, 10*, 58–89.

Smith, J., Meyers, J., & Burkhalter, A. (1992). *Communicate: Strategies for international teaching assistants*. Englewood Cliffs, NJ: Prentice Hall.

Smith, K. S., & Simpson, R. D. (1993). Becoming successful as an international teaching assistant. *Review of Higher Education, 16*, 483–97.

Zimmerman, S., (1993). Perceptions of intercultural communication competence and international student adaptation to an American campus. *Communication Education, 44*, 321–335.

Chapter 6
Lecturing and Group Discussion

Lecturing is primarily a teacher-focused activity even though it can (and often should) include discussion. Small group discussion can be combined with lecture or used alone as a means to convey course content. Group discussion can occur between two students (dyad), among members of a small group, or among members of your entire class in the form of open discussion. Facilitation typically means guiding your students toward a designated end, as well as a particular level of understanding by asking leading questions, offering scenarios or activities developed to enhance their understanding of a concept or procedure.

Students learn through active engagement. As a result, sitting and listening passively to information which is conveyed solely by lecture does not promote the internalization of concepts. However, you will encounter material which should be taught to your students in lecture format. The next section will address how to maximize the lecture followed by a discussion of engaging yourself and your students in group discussion.

Lecturing

According to Lowman (1995), there are many forms of lecture including formal oral essay, expository, lecture-demonstration, lecture-discussion, lecture-recitation, and lecture laboratory. Formal oral essays involve writing out what you want to say and reading your comments to your students. Expository lectures define and set forth information. Whether a lecture is referred to as demonstration, discussion, recitation, or laboratory depends upon whether the instructor uses props to illustrate points; encourages students to make comments, express concern, and raise questions; has students read their prepared materials out loud; or, follows the lecture by having students independently work on experiments or other projects.

You will most likely engage in lecture-discussion. As you prepare, be sure to organize your material in logical units and, when addressing your class, provide them with an overview of the class period. Tell them what key areas will be addressed. Address relevance, saying why it is important to learn this information and how students can use it. Occasionally, ask them to tell you why the information is relevant.

Include examples to illustrate the topics under review. Using examples will move the subject matter from the realm of the abstract into the concrete (think of Hayakawa's ladder of abstraction). As you prepare your comments, make notes in the margin where you can ask your students for examples. You can even provide your students with an opportunity to ask (or answer) a question or two by placing them in dyads or triads and asking each group for a response. Variety will keep your students focused on the content of your lecture.

Be lively and interested in the material yourself. If you are not interested, why should your students care? Use visual aids, such as overhead transparencies, PowerPoint presentations, handouts, and the blackboard, to make it easier for students to follow your points. You do not have to review every point in the assigned readings. But you can integrate materials from sources which students have not been assigned to read. When deciding on lecture material consider the following:

- o   What are the most important points?
- o   What information might be difficult for students to grasp without your assistance?
- o   What information might they use often?

If you expected students to read an entire set of material even though you will only cover a portion in class, make that expectation clear. Also make examination expectations clear. If you are not covering material in class but it will be on the exam, they need to know. Offer to take questions on assigned reading, which will not be covered in class, *during class* as well as during office hours. Make it clear you welcome questions and will provide clarification. At the beginning of each class period, routinely ask if anyone has questions.

Do not create a constant barrier between you and your students by staying behind the podium. As you move away from the podium and in front of or among your students, you must be aware of proxemics and your students' desire that you not invade their intimate space. Also carefully consider touching. What you might consider a friendly hand on the shoulder may be interpreted as offensive, inappropriate touch by your student-especially one of the opposite sex (although this may still be the case when gender is the same).

Do not solely lecture every class period or students who enjoy interaction with their peers will feel stifled. Ideally, once you have determined the personality of your class, you will be able to vary your style of presentation to meet the needs of most of your students. Just as one form of testing (for example, only essay) is undesirable given varying learning styles, the same is true for the presentation of content. Now let us turn our attention to handling group discussion.

Group Discussion

It is important that you understand group dynamics in order to facilitate instructor lead discussion as well as to assist your students with actively and effectively participating in small group work. Be familiar with the advantages and disadvantages of group discussion. The advantages include: leadership development, generating more information and knowledge, co-creating meaning, and personal satisfaction. The disadvantages include: time-consuming interactions, inequitable contributions to the assigned tasks, and dominating personalities monopolizing the group decision process.

Types of discussion. You should also be familiar with types of group discussion, leadership style, leader responsibilities, differences in member communication styles, and leader preparedness. As you personally move your classes through discussion periods, your students will look to you to keep the discussion on track, acknowledge speakers, make internal summaries of key points and so forth. However, when you have your students working in small groups they will likely present final reports, panel discussions, or symposiums (Jaffe, 1998; Verderber, 2000). Final reports involve one member speaking for the group, panels entail several participants discussing a topic under the direction of a group leader, and symposiums allow each group member to present one part of the topic followed by moderated discussion among the group members and their audience.

Leadership styles. You should make your students aware of several leadership styles and discuss the advantages and disadvantages of each style and the appropriateness of each style given the particular class assignment which you have in mind. Lumsden and Lumsden (1996) discuss six leadership styles: laissez faire, authoritarian, democratic, transitional, transformational, visionary. Laissez-faire leaders are informal and allow the group to do whatever it desires; authoritarian leaders want complete control; democratic leaders facilitate discussion and ensure that every member's opinion is voiced; transactional leaders avoid coercion and use rewards to motivate the group; transformative leaders inspire members to meet both personal and group goals, and they provide the group with outlook. Finally, visionary leaders are change agents who set the future direction for the group or organization. Leadership styles may also be conceptualized as task or person-oriented (Verderber, 2000). The surfacing of any particular style will obviously be influenced by whether the group will be together for the short- or long-term.

Leadership responsibilities. Leadership can be emergent, designated, shared, or elected. Whether you designate group leaders in your class, or allow the group to make that determination, should depend on the maturity level and personality of your class. In either case, the responsibilities of the group leaders should be clear. Group leaders must maintain a good working environment for the group by acknowledging the contributions of each group member, giving each member an opportunity to voice opinion, managing conflict, encouraging trust and openness, and understanding the role cultural diversity plays in group interaction. According to Lumsden and Lumsden (1996), effective teams manifest:

- o Vision.
- o Goal-orientation.
- o Commitment.
- o Diversity.
- o Open communication.
- o Creative and critical thinking.
- o Culture and image.
- o Cohesiveness.
- o Synergy.
- o Syntality (group personality).

(See also Chapter 12 in Lumsden & Lumsden (1996), pp. 299–301, for more on the characteristics of effective, responsible leaders.)

Group diversity. In order to create a good working environment, a good leader is aware of how culture may influence interaction between and among group members. The leader should determine members' perceptions of how group should function—for example, individualistic versus collective goals. An effective leader will also recognize that females may engage in what Deborah Tannen (1990) refers to as "rapport talk" whereas men in the group might predominantly express themselves using "report talk." Tannen's research indicates that women can and do explain themselves but they are not usually given the opportunity to do so as men engage in domineering talk such as interrupting, controlling the topic, and giving long explanations. A savvy leader will understand as Jaffe says, that "cultures vary not only in the value they place on public speaking but also in the who, how, and what they consider normal in public speaking" (1998, p. 45). Leaders should be willing to ask their group members how they want to proceed, co-create group norms for speaking, and collaborate about the overall group goal and the corresponding objectives.

Leader preparedness. When major, long-term assignments are given to your students, you must emphasize the importance of leader preparation. (Note: You must also consider whether your leaders will receive additional points considering their expanded responsibilities.). Verderber (2000) suggests that leaders build credibility by:

- o Being knowledgeable about the task at hand.

o   Working harder than anyone else in the group.
o   Being personally committed to the group's needs and goals.
o   Being willing to be decisive during key moments.
o   Interacting freely with others in the group.

Verderber (2000) also notes that men and women are equally capable of leading groups and engaging in activities such as planning the agenda, asking questions, keeping the group on track, and summarizing frequently. As stated earlier, you need to keep this information in mind as you plan to personally facilitate group discussion in your classes and when you setup the parameters for small group work among your students.

Part of your preparedness as the course instructor involves keeping in mind that some students prefer lecture while others love group discussion. Group discussion may leave the lecture-oriented student with an incomplete set of notes and, consequently, stressed or irritated. Conclude each class period with an overview of the key issues, questions and points that surfaced during the discussion, or begin the following class with such a review.

Cited Readings

Jaffe, C. (1998). *Public speaking: Concepts and skills for a diverse society.* Belmont, CA: Wadsworth.

Lowman, J. (1995). *Mastering the techniques of teaching* (2nd ed.). San Francisco: Jossey-Bass.

Lumsden, G., & Lumsden, D. (1996). *Communicating with credibility.* Belmont, CA: Wadsworth.

Tannen, D. (1990). *You just don't understand: Women and men in conversation.* New York: William Morrow.

Verderber, R. F. (2000). *The challenge of effective speaking* (11th ed.). Belmont, CA: Wadsworth.

Recommended Readings

Bligh, D. A. (2000). *What's the use of lectures?* San Francisco: Jossey-Bass.

Book, C. L. (1990). Extended discourse. In J. A. Daly, G. W. Friedrich, & A. L. Vangelisti (Eds.), *Teaching communication: Theory, research, and methods* (pp. 279–291). Hillsdale, NJ: Erlbaum.

Brookfield, S. D., & Preskill, S. (1999). *Discussion as a way of teaching.* San Francisco: Jossey-Bass.

Chen, G., & Starosta, W. J. (2000). *Communication and global society.* New York: P. Lang.

McCullough, M. (1998). *Black and white women as friends: Building cross-race friendships.* Cresskill, NJ: Hampton.

Nyquist, J. L. & Staton-Spicer, A. Q. (1979). *The instructional discussion methods.* Seattle: University of Washington.

Orbe, M. (1995). Intergroup relations in the classroom: Strategies for cultivating a sense of true community. *Journal of Intergroup Relations, 22,* 28–38.

Orbe, M., & Harris, T. M. (2001). *Interracial communication: Theory into practice* (1st ed.). Belmont, CA: Wadsworth.

Chapter 7
Grading Oral Performance

As you design your course, in addition to considering how to lecture and facilitate group discussion, you must also establish criteria for grading your students' formal presentations and group reports. You should also be prepared to address student communication apprehension. Above all else you should be modeling the effective speaking and confident demeanor which you expect from your students.

Formal Presentations

Whether you have complete autonomy in your classroom to determine student assignments or they are required by your basic course director or campus general education committee, you should determine the purpose for asking students to deliver oral presentations. If you are not teaching public speaking, what is the value in assigning oral presentations? You must also be prepared to respond to this question from your students.

Everyone, including you, should understand the purpose of the oral presentations and the type of presentation expected-informative, celebrative, persuasive, demonstrative, and so on.

When establishing the criteria for grading formal presentations you must be able to inform your students about the following:

o The expected type of speech and the rationale for the assignment.
o The expected length of the speech-including a minimum and maximum time.
o The weight which will be given to content and delivery-this is particularly true if student are expected to give several formal presentations.
o Your expectation regarding the use of notes and visual aids as they speak.
o Your expectation regarding submission of a speech outline. (You should review outlining rather than assuming that your students know how.)

The expected components of each type of speech and suggested assessment forms can be developed by reviewing the suggestions offered by in the instructor's manual which corresponds with your required communication text. In addition, locate sample student speeches offered by Wadsworth. These student speeches can be used as exemplars of effective and ineffective speeches. In your role as teacher, there are a number of other considerations such as classroom management, establishing your grading criteria, teaching students to reduce communication apprehension, and assessing group work. [Note: Refer to the recommended readings at the end of Chapter 5 for direction when working with English-as-a-Second-Language (ESL) students.]

Classroom Management

You must establish an environment where you students feel comfortable giving formal presentations. A comfortable environment means that both the speaker and listeners are adhering to a prescribed set of expectations. In the case of the listeners, you expect them to be in class on time, attentive, willing to ask questions, and able to provide constructive criticism when asked. Even when listeners disagree with the speaker, you must communicate that you expect them to be respectful and to avoid ad hominem attacks—keeping their focus on the content rather than the speaker. In regard to your speakers, you want them to be willing to abide by the general assignment parameters pertaining to speech length and attendance on their assigned speech day.

Time limits. For instance, if you impose a maximum speaking time, will you notify your students they are expected to stop if they exceed the designated grace period—for example, 30 seconds? It is imperative that you create a reasonable speech schedule. It is not fair to students to be delayed a class period because you did not ask a long-winded student to conclude or you scheduled far too many speeches during one class period. As a result, you should determine the maximum speech time including the point at which you will ask a student to be seated, any setup time for visual aids, settling in time at the beginning of class, and question/answer periods between or after speeches. All of these factors should be considered when determining how many speeches may be reasonably presented and critiqued during a class period.

- o   Your students will be nervous and should not be expected to keep track of their speaking time. Ask students who are not scheduled to speak to serve as timekeepers.
- o   Be sure your timekeepers understand:
- o   The speaker will need to know whether the order of the cards means time at the podium speaking thus far or time remaining.
- o   They should sit where the speakers can see them and be certain the speaker sees the movement of time as represented by the cards.

- o Not to engage in disruptive, jerky movements such as waving the time cards in front of the speakers face or lifting them above the timer's head!
- o They should signal you when a speaker approaches maximum time.
- o The importance of accurate timing of the speeches as the grades of their peers are at stake.

In this latter case, you should be open to student complaints regarding inaccurate time. Be sure you select trustworthy students to serve as timers. In some cases, you may want to have a stopwatch discreetly running for each speech yourself. With experience, you will be able to gauge a speech that is too short or too long, even without a stopwatch.

Ask for volunteers to serve as timekeepers and rotate the responsibility so no single student has the task at all times. Serving as timekeeper removes the opportunity to concentrate on and learn from the structure, delivery, and content of the work of peers. Being the sole timekeeper also reduces the student's ability to enjoy the work of classmates.

Addressing no-shows. Your policy regarding speakers who are not in class on their assigned day to speak should be clear. This policy should be articulated when you distribute the speaking assignment and should be reinforced throughout the scheduled speaking days. Your policy should be a reasonable one so you can actively enforce it without making a series of exceptions. You may indicate that documented, excused absences will be fit into the speaking schedule if you are contacted in advance. Speakers with unexcused absences might be fit into the schedule as time allows with a penalty assessed against the speech grade.

Structuring formal presentations so that students know the day and order they are speaking may reduce the problem of no-shows. Allowing students to trade speaking days (when it does not disrupt the nature of the assignment) may also reduce the likelihood of schedule conflicts and students' failing to show for their presentations. If visual aids are required, knowing exactly when they will speak is extremely important for your students. In some cases, students may have to make special arrangements to travel with and store any visual aid.

Facilitating Speaking Days

You should arrive early and request that students who have visual aids, which require assembly or special setup do so as well. Try to schedule these students early in the speaking order). You should know who is scheduled to speak and in what order and this information should be confirmed with your students. A timekeeper should be selected. You can take roll and make announcements, then proceed with the scheduled speeches.

You need to make a decision regarding how you will provide feedback to your student speakers. Some feedback should be given—how much and by whom is up to you as the instructor. There are advantages and disadvantages to providing feedback immediately after each speech, at the end of the class period, or at the end of all of the speeches. Regardless of when you decide to provide feedback, be mindful that you:

- o   Find something positive to say about the speech.
- o   Limit your comments to stay on schedule.
- o   Limit the question and answer period to stay on schedule.
- o   Model constructive critiquing behavior before expecting your students to perform peer assessment.

Addressing Communication Anxiety

Students will inevitably be nervous about delivering their speeches just as you feel anxious about your lectures and facilitations. The level of nervousness can range from normal anxiety to absolute terror. Speakers typically become nervous thinking about the act of speaking (cognitive) or while speaking (behavioral). Hamilton (1999) refers to situational and trait anxiety: nervousness stemming from a specific situation (for example, speaking in front of your church) as distinguished from the jitters associated with the discomfort of speaking in general. Whether your students' nervousness is situational or trait-based, you will be able to assist most of them.

Begin by having your students complete the Personal Report of Communication Apprehension (PRCA) form (see Hamilton, 1999; Jaffe, 1998; and, Wood, 2000). After they complete the PRCA, discuss the following suggestions for reducing anxiety:

Relax. Take deep breaths and use deep muscle relaxation. See pp. 49–50 in Lumsden and Lumsden (1996).

Visualize success. Students can engage in positive self-talk, what Jaffe (1998) refers to as internal monologuing. They can refocus negative mental pictures, and cease comparisons with other speakers.

Understand listening. Students should organize the parts of their speech and their visuals to maximize student attention and interest.

Practice. Students should set goals for themselves as speakers. After presentation, they should affirm how closely they came to accomplishing their goals and revise them for future presentations.

Incorporate visuals. Students should consider the use of visuals as one means of obtaining and maintaining audience attention and increasing their audience's understanding of the material presented.

Be attentive. As students speak, they should focus on the verbal and non-verbal responses of their audience. Student speakers should look for nonverbal confirmation that their message is understood.

In some cases, your students' uneasiness will be so great—Verderber (2000) refers to this condition as "persistent nervousness"—they will need to enroll in specialized programs for assistance. When faced with a highly anxious student, consult your basic course director to identify available resources.

Grading

Factors such as speech time limits and penalties for students who do not deliver their speeches on the assigned days would affect grading. However, consider other factors, too, when establishing criteria, assigning, and returning grades to your students.

Criteria. Specific criteria must be discussed with your students well in advance of the scheduled speech days. When discussing expectations, you should ideally provide a handout which your students can use for reference. When reviewing expectations, discuss whether you will assess your students' effectiveness based on the presence of some characteristics in their speech and delivery, combined with its overall impression. As a novice teacher, however, it is advisable to be as specific as possible regarding how you will grade your students. You may, for instance, decide to provide students with a copy of the actual form you will use when listening to their speeches. The assessment form could then be divided into the sections of the speech with corresponding points such as:

Introduction   (35 points)

Attention-getter

Credibility building statement

Audience appeal

Central thesis and Preview

An alternative system might look like this:

Introduction	(Total Possible: 35 points)
Attention-getter	10 points
Credibility building statement	5 points
Audience appeal	5 points
Central thesis	5 points
Preview	10 points

Remember the more specific the breakdown, the more cumbersome the grading process can become.

Your speech assessment form should include a section for general comments. You could divide the form into a section to note what the student did well. A second section could be devoted to noting areas that need improvement in future presentations.

Additionally, you should consider whether to include space to note the absence of an assigned speaking outline, failure to stay within the designated time limits, late speeches, and so on. In other words, consider whether you want a penalty section on your assessment form. Finally, remember to consider and equip your students with strategies for reducing speaking anxiety.

Criterion versus norm-referenced grading. Because your students will enter your classroom with varying degrees of capability, it is tempting to grade them based on how well they improve over the course of the term. Grading based on individual improvement from assignment-to-assignment is referred to as norm-referenced grading. Grading based on a set of criteria applied to all students is referred to as criterion-based grading. I strongly recommend the use of criterion-based grading.

With criterion-based grading, you can still track a student's progress from speech to speech (if you keep copies of your assessment forms) and you can note the improvement on each progressive evaluation. However, all of your students would be expected to work to meet the established criteria in order to earn a B, C, and so forth. Grading students individually may decrease class morale and create an atmosphere of friction. The disagreement would be based on more capable students noting the marked difference in their performance while other students earn the same high scores. As a result, you may not be perceived as fair and this perception can manifest itself in a hostile classroom environment. This would affect your final teaching evaluation for that term. In addition, it would be time consuming to keep track of the individual progress of a large number of students.

Returning Grades

You may not want to try to assign a grade for each speech at the end of the class period. This is especially true if you are inexperienced in grading speeches. Assign a tentative grade based on your overall impression (C, for example). Review your criteria and listen to the audiotape before finalizing the grade. Grading any assignments will take you more time while you are learning whether your criteria is appropriate based on your students' capability.

Because your impression is tentative (and you have heard several speeches) do not discuss grades with students immediately after class. What you say was an *excellent* speech may not have met some of the expected criteria and, thus, becomes a *good* speech when you apply your previously announced grading standards. Be careful not to put yourself in an awkward position.

Keep copies of your evaluation forms to track students' progression. Make notations on their assessment forms. Show them that you are paying attention to their efforts or lack of effort. When you move back into lecture-discussion, include examples of excellent student work in your class discussion and lecture. You can build self-esteem by mentioning student names. If you choose to praise particular students, at some point in the term be sure to find something good to say about each of your students. If your attention and comments are focused exclusively on one or two students, others may lose motivation and justifiably believe that their efforts and improvements are being ignored.

Small Group Work

When assigning small group work, just as you did with assigning formal presentations, you must ask foundational questions. What is the purpose of using a group format for this assignment? Do you want your students to get to know each other? Do you believe the group interaction will allow them to facilitate each other's learning? Is it important for students to take responsibility for teaching themselves the material? Even if small group work is assigned because it is expected by your basic course director, decide for yourself why the activity is justified, how to structure it and if a grade is appropriate.

Your students must be informed whether their end product is expected in the form of a final oral report, panel, or symposium (see Chapter 6). If you have not discussed the characteristics of effective speaking and the components of a basic speech (for example, introduction, body, and conclusion), then these topics must be covered as you discuss the desired small group work. Your students should be aware of the three major parts of a speech—even though they may be greatly abbreviated given the type of discussion which you might be expecting. For example, do you expect your group leader to introduce the group's position, present the key points, and then provide a concrete ending? You may want to discuss how group reports may be conceptualized as abbreviated versions of longer, more formal presentations.

The likelihood of a quality product (for example, group report, paper, and so on) can be increased by providing clear expectations and giving your students some sense of the purpose of the assignment. Consider the following:

o   Model your perception of an effective group interaction as you facilitate open class discussion.
o   Provide your students with examples of written work submitted by students (be sure to have permission) during previous terms.
o   Inform them whether or not the group project is long-term.
o   Explain whether students will receive individual or group grades. In either case, identify the basis for determining grades.

If you plan to assign a group grade, decide if it is possible for individual student grades to be lower or higher than the group based on the quality (or absence of quality) for each person's contribution to the presentation or paper.

Students need to know if you are expecting some written work and how much both the oral and written portions of the assignment are worth. Of course, they will need to know the criteria you will use to determine a grade.

Small group work is difficult to assess. Each member of the group may not contribute equally or the same quality of work to the assigned project. If the group work is done primarily in class—and your class is relatively small—you can move from group-to-group to listen in on student contributions. In addition, you can stand back from the class and note who is speaking. However, the latter situation, can be misleading. The most talkative students are not the ones who necessarily make substantive contributions.

If your criteria is nebulous for assessing group work, you are heading for a difficult situation in the form of numerous grade complaints. You should seek the advice of your basic course director and your more experienced peers in setting up the specific assignment and the corresponding grading criteria. You may want to consider structuring your assignments so most of the course grade is based upon individual performance (exams and papers, for example) while only a portion is based upon group interaction. Another option is to use group work only as a means for illustrating class concepts. In this case, you would score group work simply as the presence or absence of the student on the days of scheduled group exercises while noting, if relevant, the thoroughness of the group leader's summary.

Cited Readings

Hamilton, C. (1999). *Essentials of public speaking.* Belmont, CA: Wadsworth.

Jaffe, C. (1998). *Public speaking: Concepts and skills for a diverse society.* Belmont, CA: Wadsworth.

Lumsden, G., & Lumsden, D. (1996). *Communicating with credibility and confidence.* Belmont, CA: Wadsworth.

Verderber, R. F. (2000). *The challenge of effective speaking* (11th ed.). Belmont, CA: Wadsworth.

Wood, J. T. (2000). *Communication in our lives* (2nd ed.). Belmont, CA: Wadsworth.

Recommended Readings

Quigley, B. L. (1998). Designing and grading oral communication assignments. In R. S. Anderson, & B. W. Speck (Eds.), Changing the way we grade student performance: Classroom assessment and the new learning paradigm. *New directions for teaching and learning* (Vol. 74, pp. 41–49). San Francisco: Jossey-Bass.

Rubin, R. B. (1990). Evaluating the product. In J. A. Daly, G. W. Friedrich, & A. L. Vangelisti (Eds.), *Teaching communication: Theory, research, and methods* (pp. 379–401). Hillsdale, NJ: Lawrence Erlbaum.

Smythe, M., Kibler, R. J., & Hutchings, P. W. (1973). A comparison of norm-referenced and criterion-referenced measurement with implications for communication instruction. *The Speech Teacher, 22,* 1–17.

Chapter 8
Discipline and Motivation

Preparation and strong interpersonal skills are key aspects to effective teaching but they are not enough. You must also learn to address the classroom discipline and motivational issues which will undoubted arise in some form as you teach. Some common issues you may face include unprepared students, talkative students, unexpected outbursts, and grade complaints (during class). In addition, your students may introduce sensitive topics and it is your responsibility to manage the conversation. Finally, there is the issue of how to address plagiarism.

Unprepared Students

Students who are unprepared can be either silent or talkative. In the case of talkative students, they are ready to contribute their thoughts even though they have not reviewed the assigned material. In both cases, you are faced with a problem-a discussion or small group activity which is going nowhere. When you have students who have obviously not read the material, you should not be sarcastic or rude. In a matter-of-fact manner, acknowledge their comments, note they are not directly relevant to the topic at hand, and open the floor for other ideas. Do not allow a person who is not on target to continue to talk. It is imperative to ensure that the rest of your students are not jotting down incorrect information or being confused. If no other student has the answer you seek, provide the students with the information they need.

The most advisable way to minimize the likelihood of unprepared students is to assign homework in advance in preparation for your desired group discussion. Depending on the general preparedness of your class, you can decide whether to attach a grade or small quiz to the assignment.

Ineffective small group discussion. Related to this issue of unprepared students is ineffective small group discussion. Try to avoid the likelihood of ineffective discussion by appointing your more reliable students as group leaders. Also avoid allowing domineering students to monopolize group discussions. (Chapter 6 discusses aspects of this). When you notice one or two students dominating a group you may want to:
- o   Move toward the group and shift attention to the comments of another student.
- o   Ask what the designated leader thinks about the matter under discussion.

- Move the more domineering personalities into a group of their own.
- Appoint a quieter student as group leader and emphasize that student's leadership role.

Finally, it is always wise to have an alternative plan. If the discussion is not going well, perhaps you need to move the class into a circle, be seated and walk them through the process. In other words, move yourself into the combination of lecturer and facilitator. You could also turn the class period into a work period in preparation for your next meeting. Be mindful, however, not to allow your students to train you to consistently do most of the work for them.

Talkative Students

Some students come to class eager to discuss the course materials while others are eager to interact and discuss the latest "happenings" with their friends and acquaintances. In either case, during the first few weeks of the term, you need to establish that order is necessary for the learning process to function at its best. You can head off problems, starting with the first class period, by indicating that class has officially begun at the start of roll call. You do not have to be rude but you can be firm. Simply state that you find it distracting to hear so many other voices as you call roll and indicate that attention is needed whether you or a fellow student has the floor.

Inevitably some of your students will want to talk anyhow. If you have one student who wants to answer every question or who constantly volunteers information, you can acknowledge the student, say you do not want them to do all of the work, and then ask other students for their input. You can then return to your talkative person after others have had a chance to speak. If the person continues to be overzealous, you may need to speak to them privately after class or during an office hour.

If you have students who are busy talking among themselves, try the following:

- Move toward your talkative students without directly calling attention to them and deliver your lecture from that position until they get the point.
- Ask those students if they would like to add to the material which you have just presented.
- Separate them during small group activities.

If the talking continues, remember that your other students are counting on you to bring order to the class. Before or after class, tell them directly that you are trying not to embarrass them by asking them to be quiet. Indicate, however, that you will do so if their conversations do not cease. If relevant, mention that their class participation score may be detrimentally affected if their distracting behavior continues. And, if matters get worse, speak to your basic course director or department chair regarding your rights as an instructor. Can you tell them to leave the classroom? Can you require that they meet with you and your basic course director or department chair? Always document disruptive behavior and your response to it and attempts to prevent it from surfacing in your class. You may need this documentation later if a complaint is filed regarding your teaching or a student's final grade.

Outbursts

There are students who talk continuously and there are those who will suddenly blurt out a comment or complaint. Just as children test their parents, students will inevitably test their instructors—especially instructors who are new to teaching. Students may rudely interrupt (or make jokes) under any number of circumstances ranging from discontent with grades to disagreement with information presented by their instructor or peers. Reducing the likelihood of outbursts pertaining to discontent about grades is addressed in the next section. Although is it not possible to cover all possible situations, some general guidelines are as follows:

o   Early in the term, establish your rules of conduct. Emphasize the importance of respectful, orderly interaction. Note the difference between differences of opinion focused on ideas versus ad hominem attacks.

o   Indicate that you want to be treated in a respectful manner and will exhibit the same respect toward students.

o   Allow your class to establish its own set of interactive expectations especially if the class content will be controversial or sensitive. This way they can claim ownership in the disciplinary process.

Verderber (1999) identifies four negative roles which can appear during group discussion: aggressors, jokers, withdrawers, and monopolizers. Verderber notes that aggressors may have to be confronted, jokers ignored, and monopolizers "held in check" if they talk too much. If outbursts do occur, you must decide whether to ignore them as atypical and temporary, address the class as a whole requesting silence and compliance with the class interactive expectations, or to directly address the students. How you respond will depend upon your interpretation of the nature of the interruption, the motivation behind it, and how to best maintain an open atmosphere in your class. Your decision will depend upon factors such as your relationship with the students at issue, their contributions to the class, and so forth.

Maintaining a sense of humor and giving the benefit of doubt may be in order during the first occurrence. However, repetitive outbursts may require consultation with those involved after class, in your office, or a general discussion (without mentioning names) about how such outbursts are affecting movement through the course material, class morale, and so on. Regardless of the site of the discussion, conclude it by indicating the desired behavior on the part of students. In extreme cases, it may be necessary to request removal of a student from your course. In such a situation, be sure to be in contact with your basic course director or departmental chair, as well as campus legal counsel.

Grade complaints. Outbursts may occur during the emotional process of returning graded assignments such as exams. Some preliminary work is necessary on your part to make this process as smooth and uneventful as possible. Consider the following:

- Before returning graded assignments indicate that you are not disseminating the documents in any particular order. In other words, do not hand out the "As" first, followed by the "Bs" and so forth.
- Put a class profile on the blackboard indicating the number of students earning each grade (see Chapter 9).
- Inform your students you are willing to discuss their grades after they have carefully reviewed the assignment and (if relevant) your comments. This means, except for computation errors in determining the final grade, you will not discuss grades for 24 hours.
- State that students who have concerns should make an appointment or see you during office hours. They should bring their assignments and come prepared to discuss why they feel they deserve higher grades.
- Do not address grade complaints in front of other students.
- Do not belittle students. When the grade is justified, be firm and clear regarding your position, then offer assistance on the next assignment if the student is willing to come by for help. Do not offer this assistance unless you mean it.
- Recognize that students have appeal rights which may involve going to your supervisor for a second review. If the student is

not satisfied at the end of your conference, inform the student of this right and where to go for additional review.

Managing Sensitive Topics

You or your students may decide to discuss controversial topics. This will be particularly true, and is the very essence of class periods which may be devoted to persuasive speaking. However, controversy and disagreement may occur at any time during the term. It is your responsibility as the course instructor to watch out for the "isms" which might enter into classroom discussion—ageism, racism, sexism and others. Students may make negative comments about you, about their peers, or about other group members who may not visibly be present within the room (for example, homosexuals). If you are offended by the language of a student or sense that others in the class are offended, consider:

- o Paraphrasing the student's comments using more acceptable terminology, then pointing out that the language described could be offensive to some. Engage your class in a discussion of terminology which will allow discussion while referring to individuals or groups in a respectful manner.
- o Acknowledge that a controversial position espoused by one of your students coexists along with other points of view. Engage your class in a discussion of some of those other points of view.
- o Do not expect individuals to "stand up for" or "represent" a co-culture (for example, women, people of color, white males) to which they belong. No student in your class should be pressured by you or the student's peers to represent an entire group.
- o Do not allow offensive comments to be made simply because it appears members of the "group" in question are not present in your classroom. Set an example for your students by discussing the strengths associated with being members of a diverse society. (See Chapter 4.)

If necessary, speak with particular students in-person and express your concern regarding the atmosphere which they are creating in your class. Indicate you want an open environment where students may speak freely yet with reasonable attention to the feelings and experiences of others.

Personal disclosure. Sometimes sensitive topics arise in the form of the disclosure of far too much personal information. This is especially true when students are asked to deliver self-introductory speeches. It is advisable for you to encourage students not to speak on topics which are too emotionally charged. If they have never addressed that emotional topic in public before, perhaps their first public speech might not be a good time.

If a student becomes too emotional after revealing highly personal information in his speech, ask if he wants to leave to compose himself and to get a drink of water. After he leaves the room, calm the class and move to the next speaker. Once the student returns, ask if he would like to try again at the end of the class period or the beginning of the next class period. In the latter case, you will have time to discuss how to adapt the student's content for the next speaking day.

There may also be instances where a student reveals what others may view as highly personal information (such as having an abortion). Let the student speak and try to acknowledge that you understand her comments. Then move the conversation back to the day's lesson and other examples. If the student continues revealing personal information and, as a result, increasingly makes you (or your other students) uncomfortable, it may be necessary to contact her to discuss the uncomfortable atmosphere on a one-to-one basis.

Plagiarism

Another form of a "sensitive" topic appears when you suspect a student of plagiarism. The best approach is to reduce the likelihood of plagiarism occurring by:

(a) Explaining to your students what it is. (b) Providing examples of how to properly cite the work of others, (c) being clear regarding department and university policies (including punishment) toward plagiarism, and (d) varying your assignments so the same topics are not in active circulation from term-to-term.

In addition, consider:

- o Asking yourself whether you clearly explained the meaning of plagiarism and how to avoid it.
- o Asking yourself if you may be unfairly suspecting a student of plagiarism based on an unfounded negative stereotype you have of this student due to some particular group membership (for example, homosexual, person of color, international student, athlete, and so forth).

Rather than accusing the student of plagiarism, you may want to ask the student to come by your office to discuss the assignment. In the case of a paper, you might ask the student to bring some of the resources used.

You may want to delay the assignment of a grade until you can speak to the student and seek assistance from your basic course director or departmental chair. Also consider:

- o Talking to your more experienced colleagues about their experiences with plagiarism and how they have addressed this situation.
- o Starting a departmental file on suspect speeches or papers which might be used by different students in different sections of your department's basic course.

When you are unsure what to do. Seek counsel from your basic course director before even assigning a grade and definitely before returning the assignment. Always know if you are expected to seek counsel in these cases and from whom. And, finally, if you determine the student has plagiarized, do you need to inform other faculty in your department of this incident? This may be relevant if the student is administratively expelled from your class and must repeat the course at a later time.

Addressing unmotivated, overly-motivated, and difficult students can be quite stressful. Just as you must prepare your class content to reduce anxiety about your performance as a teacher capable of facilitating your students' learning, you must also try to anticipate and reduce unpleasant situations. You can never completely anticipate every possibility, and your ability to address problematic encounters will increase with your exposure to the classroom and by listening to the advice of more experienced teachers. The basic rule is: Regardless of how your students might behave, conduct yourself in a professional manner.

Cited Readings

Verderber, R. F. (1999). *Communicate!* (9th ed.). Belmont, CA: Wadsworth.

Recommended Readings

Colwell, G. (1996). *You won't believe this but . . . : Responding to student complaints and excuses.* Calgary, Alberta: Detselig Enterprises.

Richardson, S. M. (Ed.). (1999). *Promoting civility: A teaching challenge.* San Francisco: Jossey-Bass.

Chapter 9
Record Keeping

Being preoccupied with preparing for your teaching and completing your own coursework is certainly understandable. However, part of your teaching responsibility includes keeping accurate records. Just stop for a moment and think how you would feel if one of your professors did not enter one or more of your assignment grades in the class grade book. Also, how would you perceive the competence of that individual? Record keeping is important in teaching because it provides the information you need to assess the performance of your students, handle discipline problems, address grade appeals, and create a class performance profile.

Creating a Grade Book

Student attendance is often one criterion for determining student participation and a corresponding grade. In some classes, students are only allowed a certain number of unexcused absences before their final grade is affected. When you call roll each day, jot down the date the student is absent. You must also make a decision whether a number of tardies will equal the equivalent of one day of absence. For example, will three tardies count as one day of absence? Be sure to emphasize that it is the responsibility of latecomers to inform you of their presence and remember that any attendance policy should be clearly stated on the course syllabus.

After you have a final roll sheet (no further adds allowed), transfer your student names (in alphabetical order) and attendance into your grade book. You will also want to leave room to enter grades as well. Rather than only entering scores, it is important to note the particular assignment and point value at the top of your grade column for each class project and exam.

Your grade book might look like this:

Sept. 14	Sept. 16	Sept. 18
Exam 1		Quiz 1
20 pts.		10 pts.

Adams, Jay   X   X

              0 F   --   4 F

Adler, May

              18 A-   --   10 A

Burns, Lee   X   X

              0 F   –   8 B

The X or a checkmark would symbolize that a student was absent on that day of class. Even when using a point system, write the equivalent letter grade next to the points earned. This system provides an easy way of visually tracking student performance in your course.

After each major graded assignments (exams, papers), provide your students with a class profile. Write on the blackboard the minimum points required for a particular grade and the number of students who earned those grades. This allows students to see the quality of the class performance in general and their performance, in particular, in comparison to others. You may want to note (if it is the case) that some student may only be a few points away from the next higher grade. The issue, for students, is then to figure out how to gain those points on future assignments.

Be sure to log grades before returning assignments to students including those graded with a check +, check, or check - system. Check your grade book regularly to be sure if you have forgotten to log grades, you can then retrieve the assignment sheet or exam from your students and enter them. Also remember to log any late assignments (for example, student with excused absence) before returning them. Another possibility involves using an Excel spreadsheet as your grade book. Using Excel or some other grading software will provide you with an up-to-date subtotal of each student's current class grade.

Final Grade Computation

At the end of the term, tally each student's scores, add any extra credit, and deduct any penalties for poor attendance. You may also need to make a judgment regarding a participation score. In the latter case, hopefully, you have already established some objective criteria (for example, quizzes, homework assignments) in addition to your subjective judgment regarding the student's level and quality of participation during lecture/discussion, small group exercises, and so forth. What ever your penalties or the criteria for a particular participation grade, apply your criteria consistently across all students.

Student grades will not always easily fall into your designated grade categories. You will undoubtedly have a few student who are borderline—meaning they are just a few points from the next higher grade. You will need to reflect (this is why record keeping is important) on student attendance, preparedness, possible instructor grading errors (maybe the student deserved another point or two but did not come by to appeal), and the amount of extra credit offered during the term. If you are having difficulty deciding whether to move a student to a higher grade, ask yourself if you gave the student an opportunity to increase her/his score which s/he chose not to take advantage of. For instance, perhaps you informed this student that you were willing to take a paper late but the assignment was never submitted. In cases such as these, it would be advisable to let the grade remain as it stands.

Discipline problems. Another gray area pertaining to grading involves what you should do with your discipline problems. You should be documenting the nature of the problem throughout the term and informing your student that her/his participation score may suffer unless their behavior improves. If their behavior does not (see Chapter 8), you may be justified in lowering that student's participation score to a "D" or even an "F" based on disruptive, unproductive behavior. In cases such as this, seek the advice of your basic course director.

You also need to know your department and campus policies regarding assigning "incomplete" grades. Does the student need to have a sudden emergency which occurs at the end of the term? When and how must the grade be made up? Would it be better for the student to request a medical withdrawal? In the latter case, ask students how their financial aid and scholarships might be affected. Again, you may want to seek advice from your basic course director regarding the best manner in which to assist your student without harming the student's academic record.

Determine the students' final grades and log them, along with the total percentage (such as 84%) in your grade book. Transfer the information to your institutions grade roster being sure to follow the directions carefully regarding whether to use pencil or ink, where to sign, and when and where to submit the forms. Always make a copy for your final class records.

The last step is to check your department policy regarding posting student grades. If you are allowed to post grades, do not use student names. In addition, do not list complete social security numbers. You may want to post grades by the last four digits of your students' social security numbers in random order. Do not follow alphabetical order and as you mix the order be careful that you are listing the appropriate grade for each student. You may also want to consider listing the percentage so students know how close they were to the next grade for example, B+, 89%.

Grade Appeals

Accurate records kept throughout the semester will reduce the number of grade appeals especially if your records are shared, at some point during the term, with your students. In addition, imposing a statute of limitation (see Chapter 7) for appeals after returning each assignment will prove helpful. Generally then, you must be prepared to discuss the grade a student has earned on the last assignment, how you have calculated the final class participation score, and any penalty points assessed.

Just as I have advised regarding grade appeals which occur after returning assignments, be open to listening to what your students have to say when asking you to change the final course grade. This does not mean you should feel obligated to change the grade but keep an open mind as there may be an error in your records or some aspect of your student's performance which you did not consider.

Should student approach you regarding the performance of other students, indicate that legally you are only able to discuss the performance of the student making the grade appeal. You may want to note there may be any number of reasons why this student's colleague received a higher grade but you are only at liberty to discuss the particular appeal before you. If you choose to change a student grade, be sure to keep a copy of the change form for your records and go back to your original records to make a notation regarding the adjustment and the rationale for it.

Creating a Class Profile

The ability to see a class profile can also provide you with valuable information regarding how to address future assignments. You should create a class profile after each grade assignment and at the end of the semester. In the latter case, the profile consists of students' final grades.

If the majority of your students earned *A* grades, ask yourself if they were hardworking, highly motivated students who wanted to excel or if you did not create assignments which challenged them. How can you adapt your assignments to be more challenging when you encounter particularly bright students in the future?

If the majority of your students earned grades of *D* and *F*, ask yourself if the assignments were too hard or if the grades are to be expected because you had unmotivated, uninterested students? Ask yourself if your grading standards are too high in comparison with your peers and other faculty in your department who teach the class. If they are not, consider keeping your standards but determining what you can do to move your students to a position of greater interest. Keep in mind while the responsibility is not totally yours, you still play a part.

After considering whether you were prepared and accessible to your students, if they do not perform well, do not be too disappointed. Remember that you are a graduate student and must maintain a high average to complete your program of study. The same may not be true of students at the undergraduate level, especially those enrolled in required classes outside of their major. Remember that all of your students do not wish to earn a grade of *A* or *B* and, in some cases, if an institution accepts a *D* as a passing grade, that will be satisfactory in the minds of some students. However, be careful not to project the blame solely upon your students without assessing your preparedness, clarity, accessibility, and fairness.

If you were not available, approachable, or willing to assist, how can you expect your students to perform well when a major source of the problem stems from you? Were you adequately prepared? Did you understand the material? If not, what kind of assistance are you seeking and how did you adjust your course to avoid penalizing your students—for example, a makeup exam?

Chapter 10
The Rewards of Self Assessment

Your institution has some form of teacher evaluation. Typically this will occur toward the end of the term. The frequency, such as every term, once a year or every other year, might vary from institution to institution so it is important to be clear how often you are expected to have your students assess your teaching. In addition, you should engage in self assessment in order to strengthen your teaching. Let us now address the formal assessment process.

Formal Assessment

Be familiar with the assessment document. Know what will be asked of your students and what the statistical overview means. Ask for a copy of the assessment form before beginning the term. Inquire whether different versions are available depending on the type of class you teach—for example, small seminars, lab sections, large group instruction. Keep this assessment measure in mind when designing your class. Do not teach solely to the items on the assessment tool, but acknowledge the importance of the instrument and work to ensure that students can see your abilities, such as strong organizational skills, during the term.

When administering the assessment tool, be sure the document is not administered when students are rushed. Perhaps it is best to administer the document at the beginning of the class period or at the end when they have at least 15 minutes to complete the form. Encourage written comments and note that you will not see student comments until well after the term is over. Follow the distribution guidelines for the evaluation. If the instructions say you should have a student administer the assessment instrument, then be sure to do so. You should not be present when students complete the document nor within hearing distance—just leave the premises.

After you have been evaluated by your students, if your instrument does not provide comparative data (for example, composite scores for your department, college, campus) then ask your basic course director or department chair where your scores fit in comparison with others. Keep in mind a number of factors including variation in the courses taught and teaching experience but, at least determine if you are within the average range of scores. If yes, continue with your planning as is. If not, review your scores carefully to ascertain areas where students perceive you need improvement. Your students' written comments may be particularly helpful.

Because the data from your formal evaluation may not arrive until you are already teaching during the following term, it is wise to obtain feedback from your students halfway through the term. Under these circumstances, the feedback can be used to make adjustments during the latter half of the term and hopefully to improve your final teaching scores if you are experiencing problems.

Mid-term evaluation. Just as students are typically given a mid-term evaluation, so should you. Prepare a document and ask your students what is and is not working for them. Based on your students' feedback, adapt your teaching accordingly and within reason. Discuss with your students what the class, as a whole, desired and what adaptations you are willing or capable of making. Asking for input empowers your students and shows concern for their learning. Be clear that you are asking for constructive feedback regarding your strengths and weaknesses. In order to encourage more honest responses, make the feedback anonymous. You might even leave the room while one student is designated to collect the responses and forward them to you.

Consider asking a peer to sit in and take notes on your performance. Make adjustments. Have your peer return to identify your areas of improvement and any areas requiring refinement.

Reflective Teaching and Self Assessment

Reflective teaching is strongly emphasized in the education discipline and introspective journals are employed as one means of promoting the reflective process. Within education, journals are believed to lead both students and teachers to greater levels of awareness and understanding (Grimmett, MacKinnon, Erickson, & Riecken, 1990; Pultorak, 1993).

Keep a journal. Your journal should contain macro and micro-level reflections. At the macro level, take note of your views regarding the teaching profession and the responsibilities of both student and teacher. At the micro-level, keep track of assignments and exercises that worked well. Note how you might modify and improve assignments that did not work as well as expected.

Devote some time after each class period to reflection. During this time consider:

- o Which students participated?
- o Whom did you overlook?

o   Who was absent? Were you notified in advance? (Check mail-
    box and phone messages.)
o   Who was prepared?
o   Did students communicate verbally and nonverbally that most
    of them understood the material?
o   Did you confirm your interpretation of these cues?
o   Do you need to present some of the information in a different
    way the next class period?
o   Should you slow down? Move a bit faster?
o   Should you use examples or material from outside of the re-
    quired readings?

At the end of the term, after completing your class profile, make time to
reflect on the semester. This reflection should include considering:

o   What changes are in order for the next term?
o   What worked well and should be retained?
o   Should the order of the material be changed?
o   Should the point scale be adjusted?
o   Were you biased in favor of particular students and against
    others? If yes, how will you work toward being fair to all of
    your students?

Devote additional time to reflection once you receive your teaching
evaluations from the previous term.

Cited Readings

Grimmett, P. P., MacKinnon, A. M., Erickson, G. L., & Riecken, T. J. (1990). Reflective practice in teacher education. In R. T. Clift, W. R. Houston, & M. C. Pugach (Eds.), *Encouraging reflective practice in education: An analysis of issues and programs* (pp. 20–38). New York: Teachers College Press.

Pultorak, E. G. (1993). Facilitating reflective thought in novice teachers. *Journal of Teacher Education, 44,* 288–295.

Recommended Readings

Boyer, E.L. (1990). *Scholarship reconsidered: Priorities of the professoriate.* San Francisco: Jossey-Bass.

Brookfield, S. (1995). *Becoming a critically reflective teacher.* San Francisco: Jossey-Bass.

Gonzalez, A., Houston, M., & Chen, V. (1997). *Our voices: Essays in culture, ethnicity, and communication* (2nd ed.). Los Angeles: Roxbury.

Campus Contacts

Compile a listing of the following campus services to assist you with questions that might arise during your teaching or record-keeping.

Audiology and Speech Pathology Department
- o   student clinic

Campus Attorney

Campus Teacher Consulting Services
- o   classroom observations
- o   student assessment recommendations
- o   new teacher training workshops

Director—Disabled Students

Library
- o   collection requests
- o   media services
- o   reference desk
- o   student seminars (library tours)

Parking
- o   parking for Disabled Students

Registrar's Office
- o   criteria for incompletes, pass/no pass, medical withdrawals
- o   student records

Student Health Services

Student Psychological Services

Index

Adams, M., 29, 30
administrative assistance: basic course director, 67
Administrative assistance: basic course director, 2, 9, 10, 11, 15, 18, 19, 24, 25, 28, 34, 35, 45, 49, 52, 53, 59, 60, 62, 63, 67, 71; department chair, 28, 59, 60, 71
Allen, R. R., 1, 3
Allen, R.R., 7
Anderson, R. S., 55
Asante, M.K., 30
assessment: self, 71; student, 48, 49, 50, 51, 55
Assessment. *See* also grading; self, 35; student, 45
Balogh, D. W., 30
Bias, 21, 26, 28, 29
Blake, C., 21, 29
Bligh, D. A., 43
Book, C.L., 43
Boyer, E.L., 75
Brookfield, S., 75
Brookfield, S. D., 43
Burkel-Rothfuss, N. L., 4, 7
Burkhalter, A., 36
Calloway-Thomas, C., 29
Campus Contacts, 76
Chen, G., 43
Chen, V., 30, 75
Class profile, 60, 66, 68, 73
Clift, R.T., 74
Colwell, G., 64
Communication anxiety, 48, *See* also Speaking anxiety
Confidence, 1, 3, 4, 6, 10, 22, 25, 54

contexts, 27
Contexts, 12; campus, 27; community, 27; department, 27
Cooper, P., 29
Cooper, P. J., 21, 29
Cross, W. E., Jr., 30
Culture, 3, 4, 22, 30, 40, 61; bias & prejudice, 21; co-cultures, 21, 24, 25; upbringing, 1, 25; world view, 2, 22
Dale, P., 36
Daly, J.A., 7, 30, 43, 55
Darling, A. L., 1, 7, 8
Department expectations, 9
Dewey, M. L., 1, 7
Discipline, 3, 5, 9, 10, 11, 13, 57; outbursts, 59, 60; talkative students, 53, 58
Diversity, 29, 30, 33, 40
Dodd, D.H., 21, 29
Erickson, G.L., 72, 74
Eschbach, K., 30
ESL students, 36, 46
Ethical behavior, 24
Fink, D. S., 4, 7
Ford-Ahmed, T., 30
Friedrich, G. W., 7, 30, 55
Friedrich, G. W., 43
Friesem, K., 36
Fuller, F. F., 3, 7
Galvin, K. M., 2, 7, 23, 29
Gomez, C., 30
Gonzalez, A., 30, 75
Grading, 17, 18, 19, 24; complaints, 47, 53, 57, 60; criteria, 49, 50, 52, 67, 76; discipline problems, 65, 67; fairness, 69; grade book, 65; oral performance, 45

Graduate teaching assistants: concerns, 1, 3; of color, 21; orientation, 9, 12

Grant, M., 36

Gray, W. S., 7

Grimmett, P. P., 72, 74

Gudykunst, W. B., 30

Hamilton, C., 48, 54

Hamlet, J., 30

Hardiman, R., 30

Harris, T. M., 43

Hendrix, K. G., 9, 16, 25, 29, 30, 36

Historically Black colleges and universities, 22

Houston, M., 30, 75

Houston, W. R., 74

Hutchings, P. W., 55

Ibrahim, F., 30

International teaching assistants, 36; first week of classes, 14; interpersonal relationships, 3; Interpersonal relationships, 25

Jackson, B. W., 30

Jaffe, C., 39, 40, 42, 48, 54

Keith-Spiegel, P., 30

Kibler, R. J., 55

Ladson-Billings, G., 30

Leadership. *See* also Small groups; preparedness, 39; responsibilities, 39; styles, 39

Lecture, 37, 38, 41, 43, 45, 48, 58

Lee, W. S., 30

Lewis, K., 30

Logan, C., 29

Lowman, J., 23, 29, 37, 42

Lumsden, D., 39, 40, 42, 48, 54

Lumsden, G., 39, 40, 42, 48, 54

MacKinnon, A. M., 72, 74

Martens, G. G., 1, 7

Martin, J. N., 31

Marty-White, C. R., 3, 8

McCullough, M., 43

McKeachie, W. J., 7, 29

Menges, R. J., 7

Meyers, J., 36

Microteaching, 12

Motivation, 11, 51; unprepared students, 57

Nadler, L. B., 7

Nakayama, T. K., 31

Non-native English speaking TAs. *See* International TAs

Nyquist, J., 30, 43

Obear, K., 29

Office hours, 10, 19, 23, 26, 34, 38, 60

Ohnishi, H., 30

Orbe, M., 30, 43

Parsons, J. S., 7

Perkins, D. V., 30

Phelps, R. E., 31

Plagiarism, 19, 57, 62

Porter, P. A., 36

Preparation, 1, 3, 4, 6, 7, 9, 10, 11, 57; leader, 40

Preskill, S., 43

Pugach, M. C., 74

Pultorak, E. G., 74

Quigley, B. L., 30, 36, 55

Raimy, V., 29

Record keeping, 65, 67; attendance, 65; discipline, 65; gradebook, 65

Richardson, S. M., 64

Riecken, T. J., 74

Rubin, R. B., 30, 55

Rueter, T., 1, 7

Ryan, M. P., 7

Sandhu, D. S., 30

Self assessment, 71; mid-term, 72; peer, 72; supervisory input, 71

Self-concept, 22

Sensitive topics (managing), 57

Simpson, R. D., 36
Small group: diversity, 40
Small groups, 39; advantages,
    39; disadvantages, 39; types,
    39
Smith, J., 36
Smith, K. S., 36
Smythe, M., 55
Socialization, 2, 7
Speaking anxiety, 50
Speck, B. W., 55
Speeches, 45; criteria, 45;
    facilitating speaking days, 47
Sprague, J., 7
Starosta, W. J., 43
Staton, A. Q., 8, 30
Staton-Spicer, A. Q., 8, 43
Stewart, J., 29

Students of color, 22, 26
Svinicki, M., 1, 8
Syllabus, 10, 33; design, 17
Tannen, D., 42
Torres, V., 31
Trank, D. M., 1, 8
Uncertainty reduction, 1
Vangelisti, A. L., 7, 30, 43, 55
Verderber, R. F., 42, 54, 64
Wander, P. C., 31
Weinstein, G., 29
Whitley, Jr., B. E., 30
Wilkinson, C. A., 29
Willer, L. R., 8
Wittig, A. F., 30
Wood, J. T., 54
Yoder, J., 30
Zimmerman, S., 36